Microsoft®
Windows 7

Prentice Hall
is an imprint of

Harlow, England • London • New York • Boston • San Francisco • Toronto • Sydney • Singapore • Hong Kong
Tokyo • Seoul • Taipei • New Delhi • Cape Town • Madrid • Mexico City • Amsterdam • Munich • Paris • Milan

PEARSON EDUCATION LIMITED

Edinburgh Gate
Harlow CM20 2JE
Tel: +44 (0)1279 623623
Fax: +44 (0)1279 431059
Website: www.pearsoned.co.uk

First published in Great Britain in 2010

ISBN: 978-0-273-72913-6

British Library Cataloguing-in-Publication Data
A catalogue record for this book is available from the British Library

Library of Congress Cataloging-in-Publication Data
Ballew, Joli.
  Microsoft Windows 7 in simple steps/Joli Ballew.
    p. cm.
  ISBN 978-0-273-72913-6 (pbk.)
  1. Microsoft Windows (Computer file) 2. Operating systems (Computers) I. Title.
  QA76.76.O63B35928 2010
  005.4'46--dc22
                    2009034616

10 9 8 7 6 5 4 3 2 1
13 12 11 10 09

Designed by pentacorbig, High Wycombe
Typeset in 11/14 pt ITC Stone Sans by 3
Printed and bound by Rotolito Lombarda, Italy

The publisher's policy is to use paper manufactured from sustainable forests.

Microsoft®
Windows 7

in Simple
steps

Joli Ballew

Use your computer with confidence

Get to grips with practical computing tasks with minimal time, fuss and bother.

In Simple Steps guides guarantee immediate results. They tell you everything you need to know on a specific application; from the most essential tasks to master, to every activity you'll want to accomplish, through to solving the most common problems you'll encounter.

Helpful features

To build your confidence and help you to get the most out of your computer, practical hints, tips and shortcuts feature on every page:

ALERT: Explains and provides practical solutions to the most commonly encountered problems

HOT TIP: Time and effort saving shortcuts

SEE ALSO: Points you to other related tasks and information

DID YOU KNOW? Additional features to explore

WHAT DOES THIS MEAN?
Jargon and technical terms explained in plain English

Practical. Simple. Fast.

in Simple steps

Dedication:

For Mom, I miss you deeply.

Author's acknowledgements:

The older I get and the more books I write, the more people there are to thank and acknowledge. I am thankful for many things, including the opportunities offered by Pearson Education every time there's a new Windows edition, and the awesome team of editors and typesetters who work tirelessly to turn my words into pages and those pages into books.

I am thankful that I have a supportive family, including Jennifer, Andrew, Dad and Cosmo. I am thankful to my extended family for all playing a role in my daughter's upbringing and success. I am thankful for my health, much to the credit of my doctor, Kyle Molen. Between the lot of them, they keep me in check, on track, healthy and sometimes even sound.

I miss my mother, who passed away in February 2009, but I am thankful that some day I'll be able to see and talk to her again, something she worked hard to make me understand shortly after she passed away.

And finally, I'm thankful to my agent, Neil Salkind, who encourages me, is my biggest fan and always has my back, no matter what. Everyone should have someone like that in their lives.

in **Simple** steps

Contents at a glance

Contents

1 Getting started with Windows 7

4 Files and folders

5 Connecting to and surfing the Internet

6 Working with email

7 Stay secure

11 Windows Media Center

12 Change system defaults

13 Create a HomeGroup and share data and printers

14 Fix problems

Top 10 Windows 7 Problems Solved

Top 10
Windows 7 Tips

Tip 1: Change the desktop background

One of the first things you may like to do when you get a new PC or upgrade an older one is to personalise the picture on the desktop. That picture is called the background. You can use a background included with Windows 7 or any picture of your own.

1 Right-click an empty area of the desktop.

2 Click Personalize.

View ▶
Sort By ▶
Refresh

Paste
Paste Shortcut

New ▶

Screen Resolution
Gadgets
Personalize — **2**

3 Click Desktop Background.

4   For Location, select Windows Desktop Backgrounds. If it is not chosen already, click the down arrow to locate it.

5   Use the scroll bars to locate the wallpaper to use as your desktop background.

6   Select a background to use.

7   Select a positioning option (the default, Fill, is the most common).

8   Click Save changes.

9   Click the red X in the top right corner of the Personalization window to close it.

? DID YOU KNOW?

You can click the Browse button to locate a picture you've taken, acquired or otherwise saved to your computer, and use it for a desktop background. Pictures are usually found in the Pictures folder.

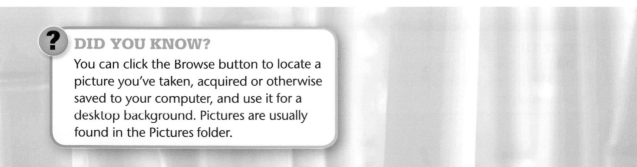

Tip 2: Use Flip 3D

Windows Flip 3D offers a quick way to choose a specific window when multiple windows are open. With Flip, you can scroll through open windows until you land on the one you want to use, then select it.

1 With multiple windows open, on the keyboard hold down the Windows key, which may have Start written on it, with one finger (or thumb).

2 Click the Tab key once, while keeping the Windows key depressed.

3 Press the Tab key again (making sure that the Windows key is still depressed) to scroll through the open windows.

4 When the item you want to bring to the front is selected, let go of the Tab key, then let go of the Windows key.

HOT TIP: The Windows key is the key to the left of the space bar and has the Windows logo printed on it.

ALERT: If Flip 3D doesn't work, or if you get only Flip and not Flip 3D, you need to enable a Windows theme in the Personalization options.

Tip 3: Write a letter with Notepad

If your word-processing tasks involve only creating a quick memo, note or letter and printing it out, or putting together a weekly newsletter that you send via email, there's no reason to purchase a large office suite like Microsoft Office (and learn how to use it) when Notepad will do just fine. You can't create and insert tables, add endnotes, add text boxes or perform similar tasks with Notepad, but you may not need to. Notepad is a simple program with only a few features, making it easy to learn and use.

1 Click Start.

2 In the Start Search window, type Notepad.

3 Click Notepad under Programs. (Note that you may see other results, as shown here.)

Programs (1)
Notepad
Documents (10)
Computer Basics Proofs
RE: boot problem
FW: TK 632 entire Chapter 4?

3

2

See more results

Notepad   ×   Shut Down ▶

ALERT: Notepad has five menus: File, Edit, Format, View and Help. After you become familiar with these menus, what you learn will carry over to almost any other program you'll use.

4 Click once inside Notepad and start typing.

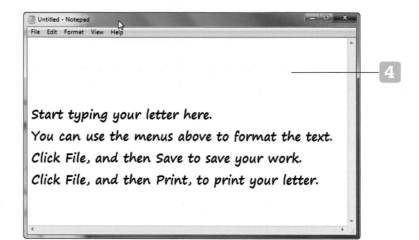

4

> Start typing your letter here.
> You can use the menus above to format the text.
> Click File, and then Save to save your work.
> Click File, and then Print, to print your letter.

? DID YOU KNOW?
The Format menu includes options for setting the font, font style, font size and more.

HOT TIP: The Edit menu lets you edit text you've written using cut, copy and paste, among other features. The Format menu lets you change the font and font size.

! ALERT: If you close Notepad before saving the file, your work will be lost!

Tip 4: Back up data to an external drive

You should learn early on how to back up data to an external backup device, like a USB flash or thumb drive or a network drive. The easiest way is to drag and drop the data.

1 Click Start and click Computer. Position the window so it takes up only about half of the desktop.

2 Locate the external drive. (Leave this window open.)

3 Locate a folder to copy. If necessary position the window that contains the folder so you can see both open windows.

⚠️ **ALERT:** Before you begin, plug in and/or attach the external drive.

🔥 **HOT TIP:** To locate a folder to copy, click Start and click your personal folder (the one with your name on it).

▶ **SEE ALSO:** For restoring a window and moving a window, see Chapter 2.

4 Right-click the folder to copy.

5 While holding down the right mouse key, drag the folder to the new location.

6 Drop it there.

7 Choose Copy Here. Don't choose Move Here. This will move the folder off the computer and on to the hard drive.

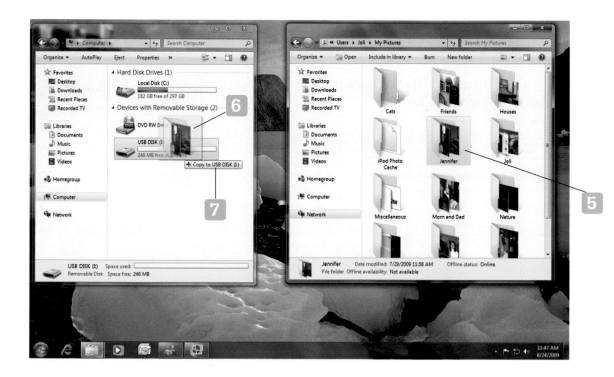

SEE ALSO: For copying and moving folders, see Move a folder in Chapter 4.

Tip 5: Download and install Windows Live Essentials

You need Windows Live Essentials. This free suite of programs includes Windows Live Mail, Live Photo Gallery, Live Toolbar and more.

1 Open Internet Explorer and go to http://www.windowslive.com/.

2 Look for the Download now button and click it. You'll be prompted to click Download now once more on the next screen.

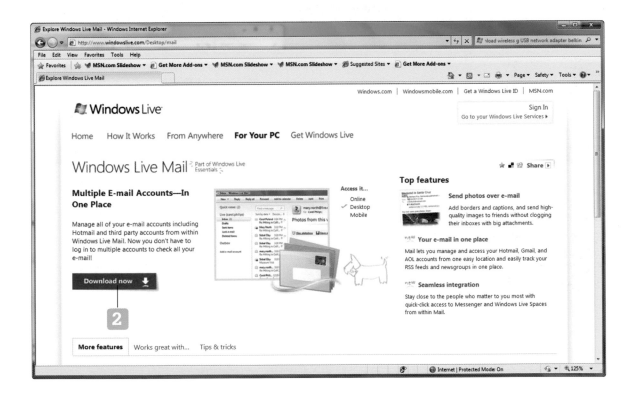

HOT TIP: Select Mail, Photo Gallery and Toolbar for best results. We'll be covering these programs in this book.

? DID YOU KNOW?
It's OK to select all of these programs if you think you'll use them – they are all free.

3 Click Run, and when prompted, click Yes.

4 When prompted, select the items to download. You can select all of the items, some of the items or only Mail. Then click Install.

5 When prompted to select your settings, make the desired choices. You can't go wrong here; there are no bad options.

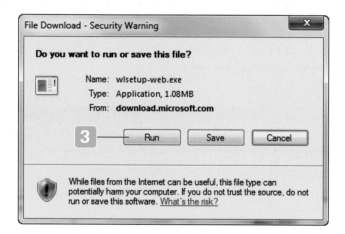

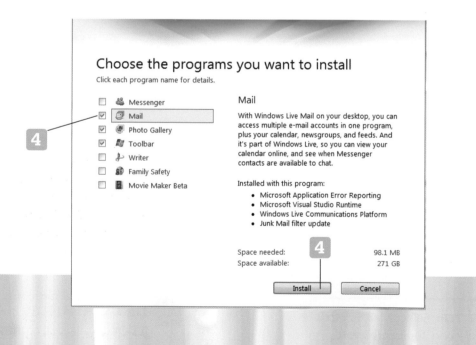

Tip 6: Get a Windows Live account

When you use 'Live' services, like Windows Live Mail, Windows Live Photo Gallery and others, you need to log in to them using a Windows Live account. A Windows Live account is an email address and password you use to log on to your Live programs on the Internet. This account is free and you can use it to sign in to Live-related websites on the Internet.

1 If you do not already have a Windows Live account, click Sign up after the installation of Live Mail completes. (You can also go to https://signup.live.com.)

2 Fill out the required information and click I accept when finished.

DID YOU KNOW?

You can use your Windows Live email account as a regular email address, or simply use it to log into Live services on the Internet.

HOT TIP: Fill out the information with true information. This is an ID, after all.

Tip 7: Add a new user account and add passwords

You created your user account when you first turned on your new Windows 7 PC. Your user account is what defines your personal folders as well as your settings for desktop background, screen saver and other items. You are the 'administrator' of your computer. If you share the PC with someone, they should have their own user account. If every person who accesses your PC has their own standard user account and password, and if every person logs on using that account and then logs off the PC each time they've finished using it, you'll never have to worry about anyone accessing another's personal data.

1 Click Start.

2 Click Control Panel.

3 Click Add or remove user accounts.

4 Click Create a new account.

ALERT: All accounts should have a password applied to them.

Guest
Guest account is off

Create a new account — **4**
What is a user account?

Additional things you can do
Set up Parental Controls
Go to the main User Accounts page

5. Type a new account name, verify Standard user is selected and click Create Account. You can click Change the picture, Change the account name, Remove the password and other options to further personalise the account.

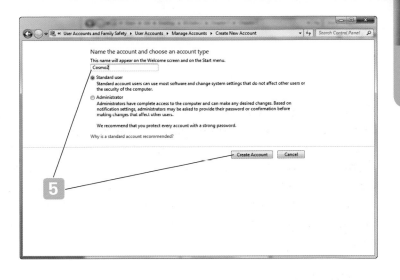

6. In Control Panel, User Accounts, locate and click the user account to apply a password to.

7. Click Create a password.

8. Type the new password, type it again to confirm it and type a password hint.

9. Click Create password.

⚠ **ALERT:** Create a password that contains upper- and lower-case letters and a few numbers. Write the password down and keep it somewhere out of sight and safe.

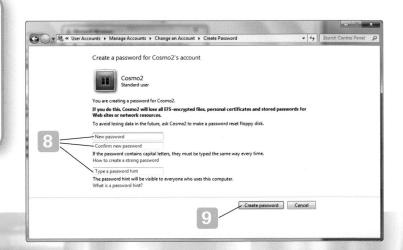

? **DID YOU KNOW?**
Administrators can make changes to system-wide settings but standard users cannot (without an administrator name and password).

Tip 8: Copy a music CD to your hard drive

You can copy CDs to your hard drive. This is called 'ripping'. To rip means to copy in media-speak. Once music is on your PC, you can listen to it in Media Player, burn compilations of music to other CDs and even put the music on a portable music player.

? DID YOU KNOW?
By default, music is saved in your Music folder.

1 Insert the CD to copy into the CD drive.

2 Deselect any songs you do not want to copy to your PC.

3 In Windows Media Player, click the Rip CD button.

HOT TIP: You can watch the rip progress in the List pane.

? DID YOU KNOW?
You have the right to rip any CD you own to your PC for no extra cost.

Tip 9: Import pictures from a digital camera or media card

After you've taken pictures with your digital camera, you'll want to move or copy those pictures to the PC. Once stored on the PC's hard drive, you can view, edit, email or print the pictures (among other things).

1 Connect the device or insert the media card into the card reader. If applicable, turn on the camera.

2 When prompted, choose Import pictures and videos using Windows Live Photo Gallery.

3 Click Import all new items now.

4 Type a descriptive name for the group of pictures you're importing and click Import.

SEE ALSO: Install a digital camera or webcam, Chapter 8.

? DID YOU KNOW?
These steps work for importing pictures from a mobile phone too.

5 View your new photos.

HOT TIP: If desired, tick Erase after importing. This will cause Windows 7 to erase the images from the device after the import is complete.

ALERT: If your device isn't recognised when you plug it in and turn it on, in Windows Live Photo Gallery click File, then click Import from a camera or scanner.

Tip 10: Disable unwanted start-up items

Lots of programs and applications start when you boot your computer. This causes the start-up process to take longer than it should and programs that start also run in the background, slowing down computer performance. You should disable unwanted start-up items to improve all-round performance.

1 Click Start.

2 In the Start Search window, type system configuration.

3 Under Programs, click System Configuration.

Programs (1)
System Configuration

Control Panel (6)
Backup and Restore
Allow remote access to your computer
View advanced system settings
Auto-hide the taskbar

Documents (23)
RE: Performance Guide review
RE: Performance Guide review
RE: Vista Trainer
FW: Doubt

Files (26)
FW: Doubt
RE: Wndows XP System Restore
RE: Wndows XP System Restore

2

See more results

system configuration   ×   Shut Down ▶

? DID YOU KNOW?
Even if you disable a program from starting when Windows does, you can start it when you need it by clicking it in the Start and All Programs menu.

HOT TIP: If you see a long list under the System Configuration's Startup tab, go through it carefully and consider uninstalling unwanted programs from the Control Panel.

4 From the Startup tab, deselect third-party programs you recognise but do not use daily.

5 Click OK.

Startup Item	Manufacturer	Command	Location
☑ HD Audio Control Panel	Realtek Semiconductor	RtHDVCpl.exe	HKLM\SOFTWA
☑ Windows Live Messenger	Microsoft Corporation	"C:\Program Fil...	HKCU\SOFTWA
☑ Windows Live Sync	Microsoft Corporation	"C:\Program Fil...	HKCU\SOFTWA
☑ SnagIt	TechSmith Corporation	C:\PROGRA~1...	C:\ProgramData

System Configuration — General | Boot | Services | Startup | Tools

Enable all   Disable all

OK   Cancel   Apply   Help

ALERT: You'll have to restart the computer to apply the changes.

ALERT: Do not deselect anything you don't recognise or the operating system!

1 Getting started with Windows 7

Introduction

Congratulations on your new Windows 7 PC – you're in for a treat and a few surprises too! Windows 7 has a ton of great features, runs faster and is easier to use than previous Microsoft operating systems. With Windows 7 (along with Windows Live Essentials), you can create text documents, upload and edit photos from your digital camera, manage and listen to music, surf the Internet, send and receive email, get up-to-the minute weather and news, and more, all without purchasing anything else.

You don't need to be a computer guru to use Windows 7; in fact, you don't have to know anything at all. Its interface is intuitive. The Start button offers a place to access just about everything you'll need, from photos to music to email, the Recycle Bin holds stuff you've deleted and you can add *gadgets* to the desktop that you'll want to access regularly, like a clock, the weather and news headlines. In this first chapter you will discover how little you need to know (and learn) to get started with Windows 7.

Important: Windows 7 manufacturers often add their own touches to a PC before they ship it. As a result, your screen may not look exactly like the screenshots in this book (but it'll be close).

Start Windows 7

Windows 7 is the most important software installed on your computer. Although you probably have other software programs (like Microsoft Office or Photoshop Elements), Windows 7 is your computer's *operating system* and thus it's what allows *you* to *operate* your computer's *system*. You will use Windows 7 to find things you have stored on your computer, connect to the Internet, have the ability to move the mouse and see the pointer move on the screen, and print, among other things. The operating system is what allows you to communicate with your PC. But before you can use Windows 7, you have to start it.

1 If applicable, open the laptop's lid.

2 Press the Start button to turn on the computer.

3 If applicable, press the Start button on the computer monitor.

3

! **ALERT:** It takes a minute or so for the computer to start. Be patient!

? **DID YOU KNOW?**
Starting a computer is also called 'booting' it.

Activate Windows 7

If this is your first time starting Windows 7 and you're on a new PC (or laptop), you'll be prompted to enter some information. Specifically, you'll type your name as you'd like it to appear on your Start menu (capital letters count) and activate Windows 7. It's important to know that activation is mandatory and it proves to Microsoft that you have a valid copy of the software.

1 Follow the directions on the screen, clicking Next to move from one page of the set-up wizard to the next.

2 When prompted to type your name and choose a computer name, remember that capital letters count.

3 Click the Start button at the bottom of the Windows 7 screen to view your user name.

? DID YOU KNOW?
Activation is mandatory and if you do not activate Windows within the 30-day time frame, Windows 7 won't let you do much of anything else *except* activate it.

Learn what's new in Windows 7

When you first start Windows 7 and click the Start menu, you'll see the Getting Started option at the top. There are several sections including but not limited to Discover Windows 7, Personalize Windows, Transfer files from another computer and Back up your files. To learn what's new, click Discover Windows 7.

1 Click Start, then click Getting Started.

2 Click Go online to find out what's new in Windows 7. Note that you'll have to be connected to the Internet to go online and find out what's new. If you're not online yet, come back to this when you are.

3 Browse through the information to see what's new in Windows 7.

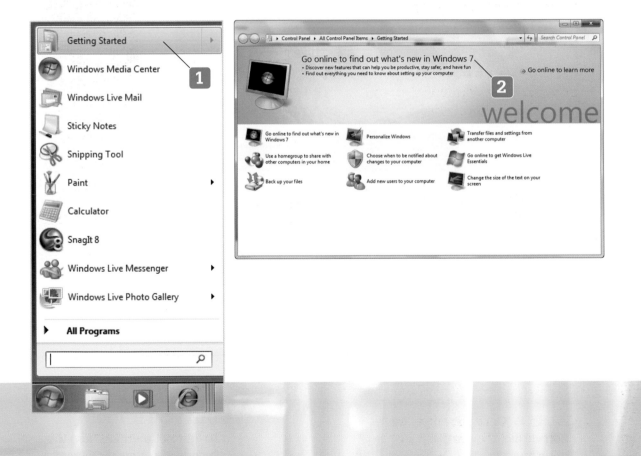

Empty the Recycle Bin

The Recycle Bin holds deleted files until you decide to empty it. The Recycle Bin serves as a safeguard, allowing you to recover items accidentally deleted or items you thought you no longer wanted but later decide you need.

1 Locate the Recycle Bin on the desktop and point to it with the mouse.

2 Right-click the Recycle Bin.

HOT TIP: You can open the Recycle Bin by double-clicking it.

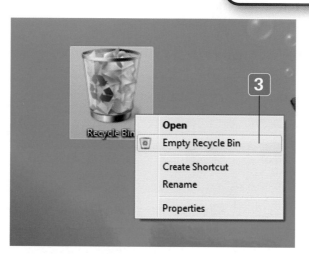

3 Choose Empty Recycle Bin.

4 Click Yes.

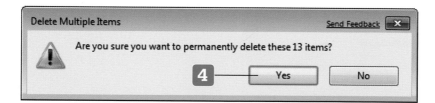

ALERT: Once you empty the Recycle Bin, the items in it are gone forever.

DID YOU KNOW?
To 'restore' anything from the Recycle Bin, right-click it and choose Restore.

Change the desktop background

One of the first things you may like to do when you get a new PC or upgrade an older one is to personalise the picture on the desktop. That picture is called the background.

1 Right-click an empty area of the desktop.

2 Click Personalize.

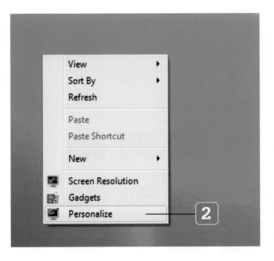

3 Click Desktop Background.

? **DID YOU KNOW?**

You can click the Browse button to locate a picture you've taken, acquired or otherwise saved to your computer and use it for a desktop background. Pictures are usually found in the Pictures folder.

4 For Location, select Windows Desktop Backgrounds. If it is not chosen already, click the down arrow to locate it.

5 Use the scroll bars to locate the wallpaper to use as your desktop background.

6 Select a background to use.

7 Select a positioning option (the default, Fill, is the most common).

8 Click Save changes.

9 Click the red X in the top right corner of the Personalization window to close it.

Change the screen saver

A screen saver is a picture or animation that covers your screen and appears after your computer has been idle for a specific amount of time that you set. Screen savers are used for either visual enhancement or as a security feature. For security, you can configure your screen saver to require a password on waking up, which happens when you move the mouse or hit a key on the keyboard. Requiring a password means that once the screen saver is running, no one but you can log onto your computer, by typing in your password when prompted.

1 Right-click an empty area of the desktop.

2 Click Personalize.

3 Click Screen Saver.

4 Click the arrow to see the available screen saver and select one.

5 Use the arrows to change how long to wait before the screen saver is enabled.

6 If desired, click On resume, display logon screen to require a password to log back into the computer.

7 Click OK.

? DID YOU KNOW?

It used to be that screen savers 'saved' your computer screen from image burn-in, but that is no longer the case.

? DID YOU KNOW?

Select Photos and your screen saver will be a slideshow of photos stored in your Pictures folder.

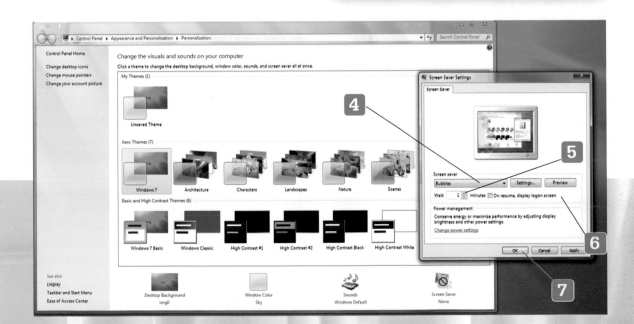

Add desktop icons

When Windows 7 started the first time, it may have had only one item on the desktop, the Recycle Bin. Or, it may have had 20 or more. What appears on your desktop the first time Windows boots up depends on a number of factors, including who manufactured and/or installed the PC.

1 Right-click an empty area of the desktop.

2 Click Personalize.

3 Click Change desktop icons.

4 Select the desktop icons you want to appear on your desktop.

5 Click OK.

Control Panel Home

Change desktop icons ——— **3**
Change mouse pointers
Change your account picture

Desktop Icon Settings

Desktop Icons

Desktop icons

4 ☑ Computer   ☑ Recycle Bin
☑ User's Files ☑ Control Panel
☐ Network

Computer   Joli   Network   Recycle Bin (full)

Recycle Bin (empty)

Change Icon...   Restore Default

☑ Allow themes to change desktop icons

OK   Cancel   Apply

5

HOT TIP: You can remove desktop icons by deselecting them here.

WHAT DOES THIS MEAN?
Icon: A visual representation of an application, feature or program.

Create a desktop shortcut for a program or application

Shortcuts you place on the desktop let you access folders, files, programs and other items by double-clicking them. Shortcuts always appear with an arrow beside them (or on them, actually). The easiest way to create a shortcut to a program (or other item) you access often is to locate it and right-click it. To create a shortcut for a program installed on your computer, you'll have to find it in the All Programs menu, as detailed here.

1 Click Start, and then click All Programs.

2 Locate the program you'd like to create a shortcut for and right-click it.

3 Click Send To.

4 Click Desktop (create shortcut).

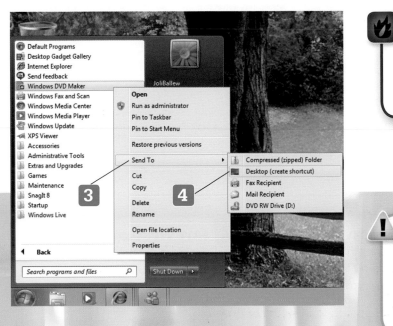

HOT TIP: You can create a shortcut for a file, folder, picture, song or other item by locating it and right-clicking, as detailed in this section.

ALERT: You can delete a shortcut by dragging it to the Recycle Bin. Be careful though: only delete shortcuts – don't delete any actual folders!

Remove icons and shortcuts from the desktop

When you're ready to remove items from the desktop, you'll use the right-click method again. The options you'll have when you right-click an item on the desktop will differ depending on what type of icon you select. You can safely delete shortcuts and Windows 7 icons like Computer and Network, but be careful that you don't delete any actual data you want to keep. Make sure you always read the warning before deleting.

1 Right-click the icon you want to remove.

2 Click Delete.

3 Read the warning and click Yes to complete the deletion.

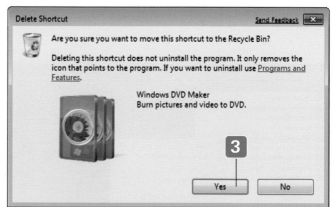

! ALERT: If you are deleting a shortcut, you might see a warning that you are moving a file to the Recycle Bin, when in reality you are not. Remember, if it has an arrow by it, it's a shortcut and can be deleted.

🔥 HOT TIP: Even if you accidentally delete something you want to keep, you can find it and restore it from the Recycle Bin.

Restore data using the Recycle Bin

If you delete something that you later decide you want to keep or need, you can 'restore' it from the Recycle Bin. That is, unless you've emptied the Recycle Bin since deleting the item!

1 Double-click the Recycle Bin.

2 Right-click the file, shortcut, folder or data to recover.

3 Click Restore.

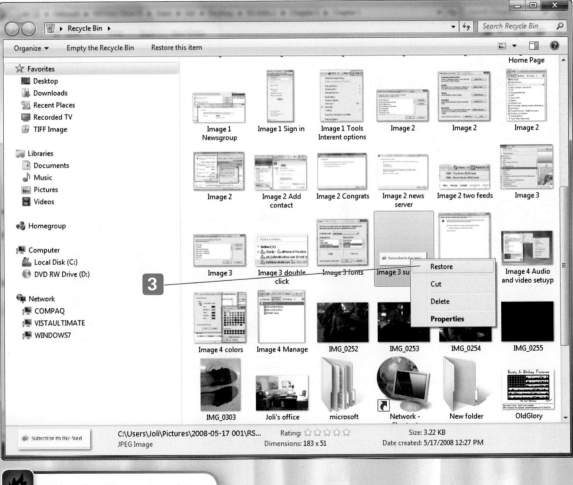

HOT TIP: The restored file will appear wherever it was saved before you deleted it.

Open your personal folder

You store the data you want to keep in your personal folder. Your data includes documents, pictures, music, contacts, videos and more. The Start menu offers a place to easily access this folder, as well as installed programs, Windows 7 features and applications (like Windows Mail and Internet Explorer), recent items you've accessed and games, among other things.

1 Click Start.

2 Click your user name.

3 View the items in your personal folder.

4 You can change how folders and icons appear in a folder by using the View menu. Here I've selected Large Icons.

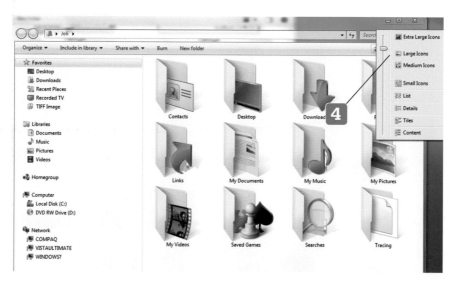

HOT TIP: Double-click any folder inside your personal folder to open it. Click the back arrow to return to the previous view (also called a window).

? DID YOU KNOW?

You can click on anything you see in the Start menu to open it and then close it using the X in the top right corner of the program window. Don't worry – you can't hurt anything!

Close a folder or window

Each time you click an icon in the Start menu, All Programs menu or on the desktop, a window opens to display its contents. The window will stay open until you close it. To close a window, click the X in the top right corner.

1 Click Start.

2 Click your user name. Your personal folder opens.

3 Click the X in the top right corner to close it.

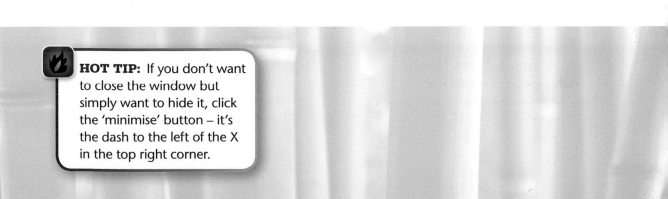

HOT TIP: If you don't want to close the window but simply want to hide it, click the 'minimise' button – it's the dash to the left of the X in the top right corner.

Open an application or program

Programs (also called applications or software) offer computer users, like you, a way to perform tasks such as writing letters or editing photos. You open programs that are installed on your computer from the Start menu. Once a program is open, you can access its tools to perform tasks. For instance, if you open Windows Media Player, you can use the interface options to listen to music, create playlists, rate music and delete music (among other things). Here you'll open the Desktop Gadget Gallery.

1 Click Start.

2 Click All Programs.

3 Click Desktop Gadget Gallery to open the application. The Desktop Gadget Gallery lets you drag 'gadgets' to your desktop. You'll learn more about this later in the chapter.

4 Click the X in the top right corner to close the application.

HOT TIP: You will open other programs in the same manner.

DID YOU KNOW?
To close most third-party programs, you can also click File and then Exit.

Search for a program

To locate a program on your computer you can search for it using the Start Search window. Just type in what you want and select the appropriate program from the list. Note that when you search using the Start Search window, all kinds of results may appear, not just programs.

1 Click Start.

2 In the Start Search window, type Media.

3 Note the results.

4 Click any result to open it. If you want to open Windows Media Player, click it once. Note that it's under Programs.

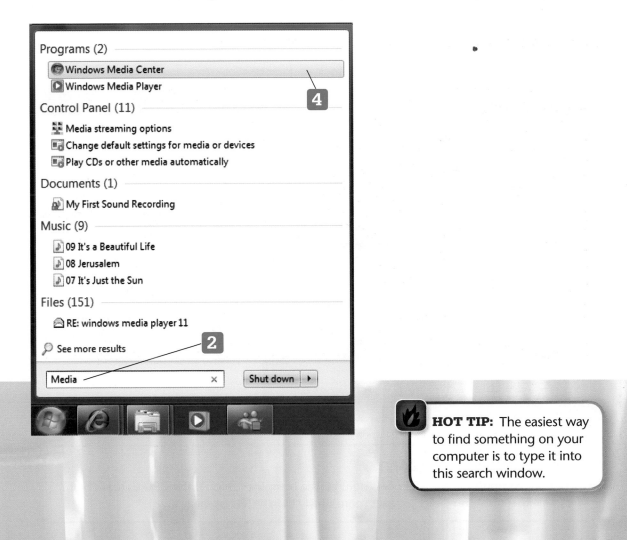

HOT TIP: The easiest way to find something on your computer is to type it into this search window.

Add a gadget to the desktop

Gadgets sit on your desktop and offer information about the weather, time and date, as well as access to your contacts, productivity tools and CPU usage. You can even have a slideshow of your favourite pictures. You can customise your desktop by adding gadgets and customising them to meet your needs.

1 In the Start Search window, type Gadgets.

2 Under Control Panel, click Desktop Gadgets.

3 Drag any gadget to the desktop. You can drag as many as you like. Drag the clock to the desktop. You'll learn to set it in the next section.

Control Panel (7)
- Desktop Gadgets **2**
- View list of running gadgets
- Restore desktop gadgets installed with Windows
- Add gadgets to the desktop
- Get more gadgets online
- Add the Clock gadget to the desktop
- Uninstall a gadget

Files (5)
- RE: Brilliant MWV for the over 50s
- RE: Windows Vista/Windows 7
- RE: Vista Trainer
- RE: 242001, Windows Vista Secrets, copyediting questions
- 342D7299-00000087

See more results

Gadgets   × | Shut down ▶

1

4 Click the X in the top right corner of the Desktop Gadget Gallery to close it.

4

Page 1 of 1   Search gadgets

Calendar	Clock	CPU Meter	Currency	Feed Headlines	Picture Puzzle
Slide Show	Stocks	Weather	Windows Media...		

Show details   Get more gadgets online

3

ALERT: You won't get up-to-date information on the weather, stocks and other real-time gadgets unless you're connected to the Internet.

WHAT DOES THIS MEAN?

CPU: Your computer's central processing unit (the computer chip). If the CPU usage is high, you can expect the computer to react more slowly than if CPU usage is low.

Set the time on the clock gadget

Almost all gadgets offer a wrench icon when you position your mouse over them. You can use this icon to access settings for the gadget. The first thing you may want to set is the time on the clock gadget.

1 Position the mouse pointer over the clock you dragged to the desktop. Look for the small x and the wrench to appear. Clicking the x will remove the gadget from the desktop. Clicking the wrench will open the gadget's properties, if properties are available.

2 Click the arrow in the Time zone window and select your time zone from the list.

3 Click the right arrow underneath the clock to change the clock type. Type a clock name if you like.

4 Click the left and right arrows to select a new clock, if desired.

5 Click OK.

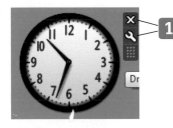

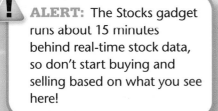

ALERT: The Stocks gadget runs about 15 minutes behind real-time stock data, so don't start buying and selling based on what you see here!

Clock

3 of 8

Next

Clock name:

Windows Clock

Time zone:

Current computer time

Show the second hand

OK   Cancel

Shut down Windows safely

When you're ready to turn off your computer, you need to do so using the method detailed here. Simply pressing the power button can damage the computer and/or the operating system.

1 Click Start.

2 Click the arrow shown here.

3 Click Shut down.

HOT TIP: If shut down is showing, you can click it directly.

? DID YOU KNOW?

Many computers now come with a Sleep button on the outside of the PC tower or on the inside of a laptop. Clicking the Sleep button puts the computer to sleep immediately. If you're taking a break, you might want to try that now instead of completely shutting down the PC.

2 Computing essentials

Introduction

To get the most out of your computer you need to understand some basic computing essentials. For example, it's important to understand what a 'window' is and how to resize, move or arrange open windows on your desktop. All of this is essential because each time you open a program, file, folder, picture or anything else, a new window almost always opens. You have to be very familiar with these windows, including how to show or hide them, in order to become comfortable navigating your computer. Beyond understanding windows though, you'll need to know how to get help when you need it, using the Help and Support Center.

Change the view in the Pictures window

When you open most folders, you will see additional folders inside them. You'll use these subfolders to organise the data you create and save, such as documents, pictures and songs. You open a folder to see what's in it and then you can change the appearance of the content inside these folders. You can configure each folder independently so that the data appears in a list, as small icons or as large icons, to name a few.

1 Click Start.

2 Click Pictures.

3 Locate the Views button.

4 Click the arrow next to Views and make a selection using the slider.

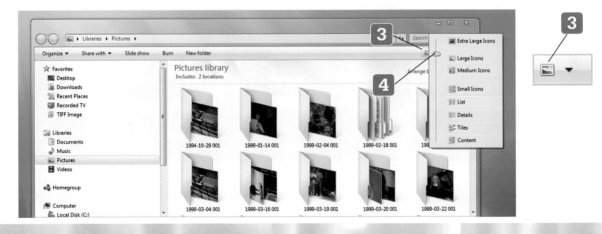

HOT TIP: Show items in the Pictures folder as large or extra large icons and you'll be able to tell what each picture looks like without actually opening it in a program.

? DID YOU KNOW?
You can also click a choice on the slider to make a view selection.

Minimise a window

When you have several open windows, you may want to minimise (hide) the windows you aren't using. A minimised window appears on the taskbar as a small icon and is not on the desktop. When you're ready to use the window again, you simply click it.

1 Open any window. (Click Start, then click Pictures, Documents, Games or any other option.)

2 Click the – sign in the top right corner.

3 Locate the icon related to the program in the taskbar. Position your mouse over the icon to see its thumbnail. If more than one window related to the program is open, you'll see multiple thumbnails. Here, Internet Explorer is selected and three web pages are open.

! **ALERT:** A minimised window is on the taskbar and is not shown on the desktop. You can 'restore' the window by clicking on its icon on the taskbar. Restoring a window to the desktop brings the window back up so you can work with it.

! **ALERT:** You won't see the thumbnail shown here unless you have a windows theme enabled. If you see only a window title and not a thumbnail, you have an 'Ease of Access Theme' applied.

Restore a window

A window can be minimised (on the taskbar), maximised (filling the entire desktop) or in restore mode (not maximised or minimised, but showing on the desktop). When a window is in restore mode, you can resize the window easily, if desired.

In order to put a window in restore mode, you have to have access to the restore button. The restore button is made up of two squares that appear next to the X in the top right corner of any window. Clicking this button will put the window in restore mode. If the icon next to the X in the top right corner of a window is a single square, the window is already in restore mode and the only thing you can do is minimise or maximise it.

1 Open a window.

2 In the top right corner of the window, locate the two-square button.

3 Click the button to put the window in restore mode.

ALERT: Remember, if you don't see two squares but instead see only one, the window is already in restore mode.

HOT TIP: When a window is in full screen mode, you can click the title bar of the window, 'shake it' by moving the window left and right, and it will automatically change to restore mode.

WHAT DOES THIS MEAN?

Taskbar: The light blue, transparent bar that runs across the bottom of your screen. It contains the Start button and the Notification area.

Notification area: The far right portion of the taskbar that holds the clock, volume and other system icons.

Maximise a window

A maximised window is as large as it can be and takes up the entire screen. You can maximise a window that is on the desktop by clicking the square icon in the top right corner. If the icon is already a square, it's already maximised.

1 Open a window.

2 In the top right corner of the window, locate the square button.

3 Click it to maximise the window.

 HOT TIP: Drag and shake any window to minimise all of the other windows automatically.

! **ALERT:** Remember, if you see two squares instead of one, the window is already maximised.

Move a window

You can move a window no matter what its mode. You move a window by dragging it from its title bar. The title bar is the bar that runs across the top of the window. Moving windows allows you to position multiple windows across the screen.

1 Open any window.

2 Left-click with the mouse on the title bar and drag. Let go of the mouse when the window is positioned correctly.

HOT TIP: Try dragging a window almost all the way off the screen to the left or right. It will automatically position itself to take up half of the screen.

? DID YOU KNOW?
You can open a document or a picture and it will open in a window.

Resize a window

Resizing a window allows you to change the dimensions of the window. You can resize a window by dragging from its sides, corners or the top and bottom.

1 Open any window. (If you're unsure, click Start and Pictures.)

2 Put the window in restore mode. You want the maximise button to show.

3 Position the mouse at one of the window corners, so that the mouse pointer becomes a two-pointed arrow.

4 Hold down the mouse button and drag the arrow to resize the window.

5 Repeat as desired, dragging from the sides, top, bottom or corners.

HOT TIP: Instead of dragging from the corners, try dragging the entire window from its title bar. Drag to the left, right, top and bottom of the screen to experiment.

Use Flip

Windows Flip offers a quick way to choose a specific window when multiple windows are open. With Flip, you can scroll through open windows until you land on the one you want to use and then select it.

1 With multiple windows open, on the keyboard hold down the Alt key with one finger (or thumb).

2 While holding down the Alt key, press the Tab key.

3 Press the Tab key again (making sure that the Alt key is still depressed).

4 When the item you want to bring to the front is selected, let go of the Tab key and then let go of the Alt key.

Sample Pictures

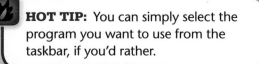

HOT TIP: The Alt key is to the left of the space bar. The Tab key is to the left of the Q.

HOT TIP: You can simply select the program you want to use from the taskbar, if you'd rather.

Use Flip 3D

Windows Flip 3D offers a quick way to choose a specific window when multiple windows are open. With Flip, you can scroll through open windows until you land on the one you want to use and then select it.

1 With multiple windows open, on the keyboard hold down the Windows key, which may have Start written on it, with one finger (or thumb).

2 Click the Tab key once, while keeping the Windows key depressed.

3 Press the Tab key again (making sure that the Windows key is still depressed) to scroll through the open windows.

4 When the item you want to bring to the front is selected, let go of the Tab key and then let go of the Windows key.

HOT TIP: The Windows key is the key to the left of the space bar and has the Windows logo printed on it.

ALERT: If Flip 3D doesn't work, or if you get only Flip and not Flip 3D, you need to enable a Windows theme in the Personalization options.

Use Help and Support

Sometimes you need a little bit more than a book can give you. When that happens, you'll need to access the Windows 7 Help and Support feature. You can access Help and Support from the Start menu.

1 Click Start.

2 Click Help and Support.

3 Select any topic to read more about it.

Windows Help and Support

Search Help

Find an answer quickly

Enter a few words in the search box above.

Not sure where to start?

- How to get started with your computer
- Learn about Windows Basics
- Browse Help topics

More on the new Windows website

Check out the new Windows website, which will soon have more information, downloads, and ideas for getting the most out of your Windows 7 PC.

More support options

Online Help ▼

 HOT TIP: Click Browse Help topics to see a list of topics you can access.

 HOT TIP: You can access the Help and Support Center from virtually anywhere in Windows 7. Look for the round blue question mark.

? DID YOU KNOW?
The Help and Support window offers an Options icon, where you can print help topics and change the text size.

3 Perform tasks with Windows 7

Introduction

Windows comes with a lot of applications, many of which may sound familiar, such as WordPad and Calculator, and some of which may not, like the Snipping Tool and the Sound Recorder. These applications, like so many others, can help you complete everyday tasks like writing and printing a letter, balancing your cheque book, taking a picture of the screen or recording a sound bite. There are games too and tools to keep your computer running smoothly like Disk Cleanup and Disk Defragmenter.

In this chapter you'll explore these features. You'll learn how to write and print a letter, for instance, and how to access and use accessories like the calculator and the Snipping Tool. You'll even learn to play a game of Solitaire on the computer.

Write a letter with Notepad

If your word-processing tasks involve only creating a quick memo, note or letter and printing it out, or putting together a weekly newsletter that you send via email, there's no reason to purchase a large office suite like Microsoft Office (and learn how to use it) when Notepad will do just fine. You can't create and insert tables, add endnotes, add text boxes or perform similar tasks with Notepad, but you may not need to. Notepad is a simple program with only a few features, making it easy to learn and use.

1 Click Start.

2 In the Start Search window, type Notepad.

3 Click Notepad under Programs. (Note that you may see other results as well.)

4 Click once inside Notepad and start typing.

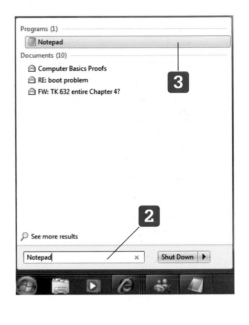

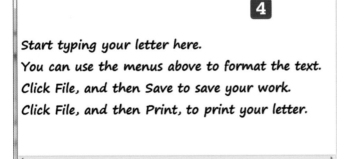

Start typing your letter here.

You can use the menus above to format the text.

Click File, and then Save to save your work.

Click File, and then Print, to print your letter.

? DID YOU KNOW?
The Format menu includes options for setting the font, font style, font size and more.

! ALERT: Notepad has five menus: File, Edit, Format, View and Help. After you become familiar with these menus, what you learn will carry over to almost any other program you'll use.

! ALERT: If you close Notepad before saving the file, your work will be lost!

Save a letter with Notepad

If you want to save a letter you've written in Notepad, you have to click File and then click Save. This will allow you to name the file and save it to your hard drive. The next time you want to view the file, you can click File and then click Open. You'll be able to locate and open your saved file using the same technique you used to save it. You can reopen a saved file and make changes to it, then resave it. Your changes will be saved as well.

1 Click File.

2 Click Save.

3 Type a name for the file.

4 Double-click the folder you'd like to save the file in (if you don't want to save the file in the Documents folder).

5 Click Save.

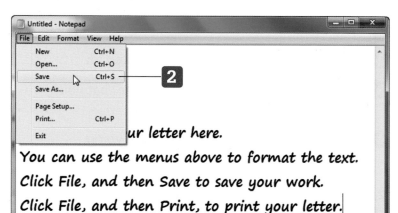

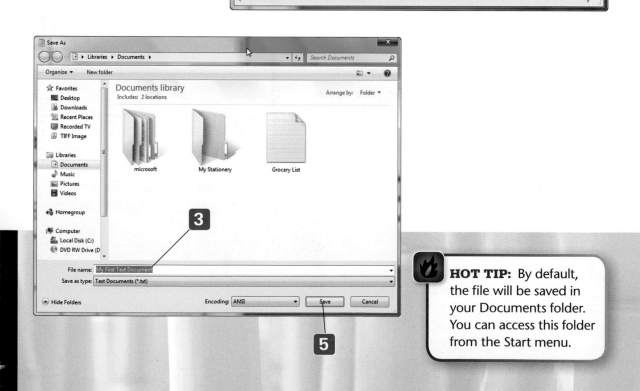

HOT TIP: By default, the file will be saved in your Documents folder. You can access this folder from the Start menu.

Print a letter with Notepad

Sometimes you'll need to print a letter so you can mail it. You can access the Print command from the File menu.

1 Click File.

2 Click Print.

3 Select a printer.

4 Click Print.

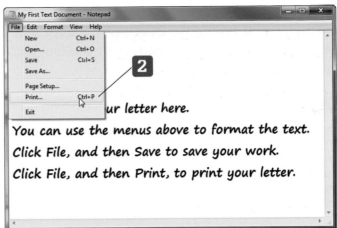

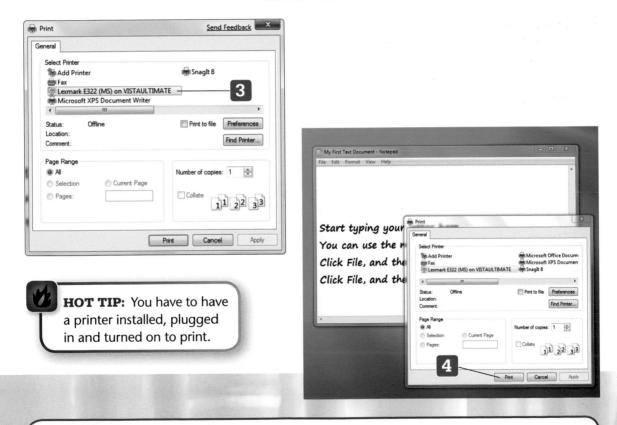

HOT TIP: You have to have a printer installed, plugged in and turned on to print.

WHAT DOES THIS MEAN?

Printer Preferences: Lets you select the page orientation, print order and type of paper you'll be printing on, among other features.

Page Range: Lets you select which pages to print.

Use the calculator

You've probably used a calculator before and using the Windows 7 calculator is not much different from a hand-held one, except that you input numbers with a mouse click, keyboard or number pad. There are four calculators available – you can switch between them from the View menu.

1 Click Start.

2 In the Start Search dialogue box, type Calculator.

3 In the Programs results, click Calculator.

4 Input numbers using the keypad or by clicking the on-screen calculator with the mouse.

5 Input operations using the keypad or by clicking the on-screen calculator with the mouse.

6 Close Calculator by clicking the X in the top right corner of it.

HOT TIP: Click View to change to a different calculator mode. Try Scientific.

Take a screen shot

The Snipping Tool lets you drag your mouse cursor around any area on the screen to copy and capture it. Once captured, you can save it, edit it and/or send it to an email recipient. There are several ways to edit the 'clip' or 'snip' (either one will do for a name for the copied data). You can start by copying it or writing on it using a variety of tools. (These tools will become available after creating a snip.) You can write on a clip with a red, blue, black or customised pen or a highlighter, and if you mess up, you can use the eraser.

1 Click Start.

2 In the Start Search dialogue box, type Snip.

3 Under Programs, select Snipping Tool.

4 Drag your mouse across any part of the screen. When you let go of the mouse, the snip will appear in the Snipping Tool window.

5 Click Tools to see the options. You can use a tool to draw on the snip.

HOT TIP: You can take a screen shot of a webpage, document, presentation or anything else showing on your screen.

HOT TIP: If you mess up, from the Tools menu choose Eraser and 'erase' what you just drew.

ALERT: If you want to keep the snip you'll have to save it. Click File, click Save As to name the file and save it to your hard drive.

Email a screen shot

You can use the Snipping Tool to take a picture of your screen as detailed in the previous section. You can even write on it with a 'pen'. You can also email that screen shot if you'd like to share it with someone.

1 Take a screen shot with the Snipping Tool.

2 Click File and click Send To.

3 Click Email Recipient.

4 Insert the recipient's name, change the subject if desired, type a message if you'd like to and click Send.

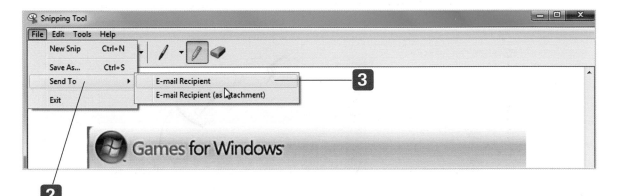

> ▶ **SEE ALSO:** For more information on sending an email, refer to Chapter 6.

> 🔥 **HOT TIP:** Emails you send can be viewed in Mail's 'Sent' folder.

> ⚠ **ALERT:** If you select Email Recipient, this will insert the snip inside an email. Note that you can also send the snip as an attachment.

Play Solitaire

Windows 7 comes with lots of games. You access these from the Games folder on the Start menu. Each game offers instructions on how to play it and for the most part moving a player, tile or card, dealing a card, or otherwise moving around the screen is performed using the mouse. One of the most popular games is Solitaire.

1 Click Start.

2 Click Games.

3 Double-click Solitaire to begin the game.

4 Double-click any card to move it or drag the card to the desired location.

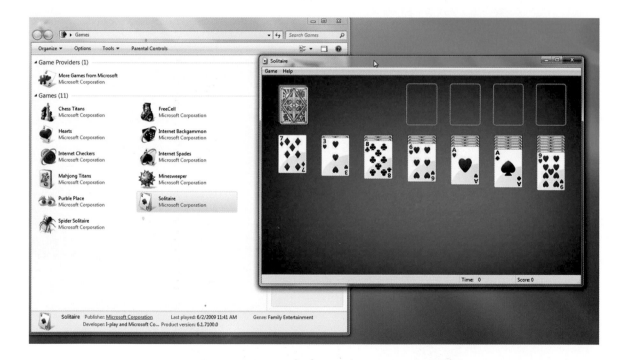

HOT TIP: Instructions will appear on the screen and you can also access instructions from the Help menu.

Record a sound clip

Need to record a quick note to yourself, a music clip, a sound or other audible? It's easy with Sound Recorder. Sound Recorder is a simple tool with only three options: Start Recording, Stop Recording, and Resume Recording. To record, click Start Recording; to stop, click Stop Recording; to continue, click Resume Recording. You save your recording as a Windows Media Audio file, which will play by default in Windows Media Player.

1 Click Start.

2 In the Start Search dialogue box, click Sound Recorder.

3 Under Programs, click Sound Recorder.

Programs (1)

🎙 Sound Recorder

Documents (3)

✉ RE: Brilliant MWV for the over 50s
✉ RE: Are you open for a question?
✉ You could get a better education fast!

3

🔍 See more results

Sound Recorder   ✕   Shut Down ▶

ALERT: You can't record anything without a microphone.

HOT TIP: You can use your saved recording in Movie Maker and other Windows-related programs and you can save and play the clip on your iPod or other media player.

4 Click Start Recording and speak into your microphone.

4

5 Click Stop Recording to complete the recording.

6 In the Save As dialogue box, type a name for your recording and click Save.

7 Click the X in the Sound Recorder to close it.

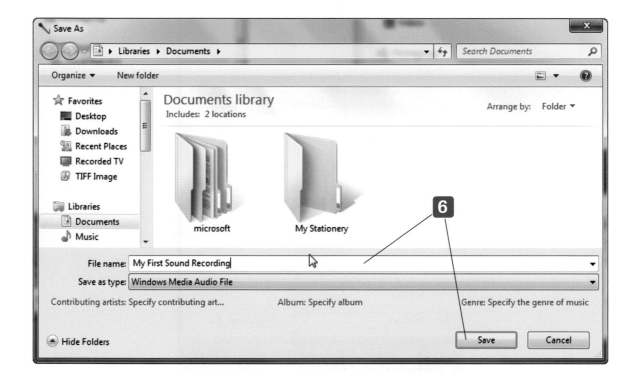

6

HOT TIP: You may want to save your recordings in the My Music folder.

HOT TIP: To play the recording in Windows Media Player, double-click it.

Use Disk Cleanup

Disk Cleanup is a safe and effective way to reduce unnecessary data on your PC. With unnecessary data deleted, your PC will run faster and have more available disk space for saving files and installing programs. With Disk Cleanup you can remove temporary files, empty the Recycle Bin, remove set-up log files, and downloaded program files (among other things), all in a single process.

1 Click Start.

2 In the Start Search dialogue box, type Disk Cleanup.

3 In the results, under Programs, click Disk Cleanup.

Programs (1)

🖳 Disk Cleanup

Control Panel (1)

🖳 Free up disk space by deleting unnecessary files

3

Documents (26)

✉ RE: System Restore!

✉ RE: System Restore!

✉ RE: System Restore!

🔎 See more results

2

Disk Cleanup | × | Shut Down ▶

1

ALERT: You may not be prompted to choose a drive letter if only one drive exists.

ALERT: If you empty the Recycle Bin all files will be permanently deleted.

4 If prompted to choose a drive or partition, choose the letter of the drive that contains the operating system, which is almost always C:, but occasionally D. Click OK.

5 Select the files to delete. Accept the defaults if you aren't sure.

6 Click OK to start the cleaning process.

Disk Cleanup for (C:)

Disk Cleanup

You can use Disk Cleanup to free up to 495 MB of disk space on (C:).

Files to delete:

- ☑ Downloaded Program Files — 0 bytes
- ☑ Temporary Internet Files — 12.6 MB
- ☐ Offline Webpages — 282 KB
- ☐ Game News Files — 2.13 KB
- ☐ Game Statistics Files — 17.4 KB

Total amount of disk space you gain: 24.6 MB

Description

Downloaded Program Files are ActiveX controls and Java applets downloaded automatically from the Internet when you view certain pages. They are temporarily stored in the Downloaded Program Files folder on your hard disk.

Clean up system files   View Files

How does Disk Cleanup work?

OK   Cancel

WHAT DOES THIS MEAN?

Downloaded program files: These are files that download automatically when you view certain webpages. They are stored temporarily in a folder on your hard disk and accessed when and if needed.

Temporary Internet files: These files contain copies of webpages you've visited on your hard drive, so that you can view the pages more quickly when visiting the page again.

Offline webpages: These are webpages that you've chosen to store on your computer so you can view them without being connected to the Internet. Upon connection, the data is synchronised.

Game news files and game statistics files: These are files related to games you've played, such as how many wins and losses you have or new information regarding the games.

Recycle Bin: This contains files you've deleted. Files are not permanently deleted until you empty the Recycle Bin.

Setup Log Files: These are files created by Windows during set-up processes.

Temporary Files: These are files created and stored by programs for use by the program. Most of these temporary files are deleted when you exit the program, but some do remain.

Thumbnails: These are small icons of your pictures, videos and documents. Thumbnails will be recreated as needed, even if you delete them here.

Use Disk Defragmenter

A hard drive stores the files and data on your computer. When you want to access a file, the hard drive spins and data is accessed from the drive. When the data required for the file you need is all in one place, the data is accessed more quickly than if that data is scattered across the hard drive in different areas. When data is scattered, it's fragmented.

1 Click Start.

2 In the Start Search dialogue box, type Defrag.

3 Under Programs, select Disk Defragmenter.

> 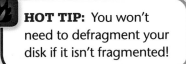 **HOT TIP:** You won't need to defragment your disk if it isn't fragmented!

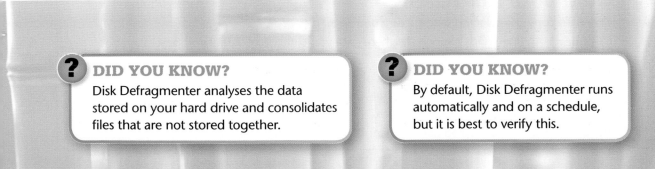

Programs (1)
- Disk Defragmenter

Control Panel (2)
- Defragment your hard drive
- Perform recommended maintenance tasks automatically

Documents (19)
- RE: O.E. INBOX LOCKUP
- RE: Stripping XP
- RE: Cleaning my hard drive

3

🔍 See more results

Defrag **2**   ✕   Shut Down ▶

? DID YOU KNOW?
Disk Defragmenter analyses the data stored on your hard drive and consolidates files that are not stored together.

? DID YOU KNOW?
By default, Disk Defragmenter runs automatically and on a schedule, but it is best to verify this.

4 Verify that Disk Defragmenter is configured to run on a schedule. If not, place a tick in the appropriate box.

5 To manually run Disk Defragmenter, click Defragment disk.

6 Click Close.

WHAT DOES THIS MEAN?

Copy: To copy the selected text, picture or object.

Clipboard: An imaginary 'clipboard' where data you cut is stored until you paste it, reboot your PC or cut something else.

Cut: To remove the selected text, picture or object and place the item on the clipboard.

Interface: What you see on the screen when working in a window. In Paint's interface, you see the Menu bar, Toolbox and Color box.

Paste: To place cut or copied data into another program, file or folder.

4 Files and folders

Introduction

You're going to have data to save. That data may come in the form of letters you type on the computer, pictures you take using your digital camera, music you copy from your own CD collection, email address books, videos from a DV camera, holiday card and gift lists, and more. Each time you click the Save or Save As button under a file menu (which is what you do to save data to your PC most of the time), you'll be prompted to tell Windows 7 *where* you want to save the data. For the most part though, Windows 7 will *tell you* where it thinks you should save the data. Documents go in the My Documents folder, Music in the My Music folder, Pictures in the My Pictures folder and so on.

In this chapter you'll learn where files are saved by default and how to create your own folders and subfolders for organising data. You'll learn how to copy, move and delete files and folders, and how to locate saved files in various ways. You'll also learn how to create a basic backup to an external hard drive, like a USB stick.

Create a folder

Microsoft understands what types of data you want to save to your computer and built Windows 7's folder structure based on that information. Look at the Start menu. You'll see your name at the top. Clicking your name on the Start menu opens your personal folder.

While Windows 7's default folders will suit your needs for a while, soon you'll need to create subfolders inside those folders to manage your data and keep it organised. You may also want to create a folder on the desktop to hold information you access often.

1. Right-click an empty area of your desktop.

2. Point to New.

3. Click Folder.

4. Type a name for the folder.

5. Press Enter on the keyboard.

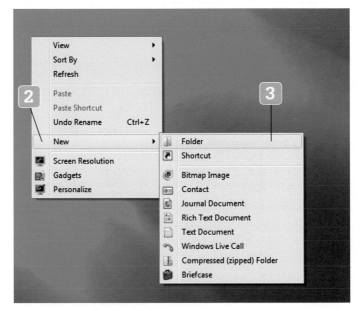

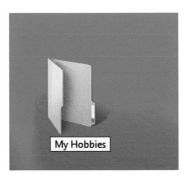

ALERT: If you can't type a name for the folder, right-click the folder and select Rename.

? DID YOU KNOW? ·

You can drag the folder to another area of the desktop or even to another area of the hard drive to move it there.

HOT TIP: Create a folder to hold data related to a hobby, tax information, work or family.

Create a subfolder

You can also create folders inside other folders. For instance, inside the Documents folder, you may want to create a subfolder called Tax Information to hold scanned receipts, tax records and account information. Inside the Pictures folder you might create folders named 2010, 2011, 2012, or Weddings, Holidays, Grandkids and so on.

1 Click Start.

2 Click your user name to open your personal folder.

3 Click New folder.

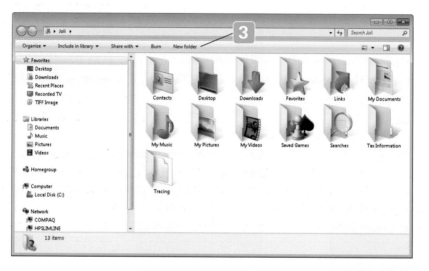

4 Type a name for the folder.

5 Press Enter on the keyboard.

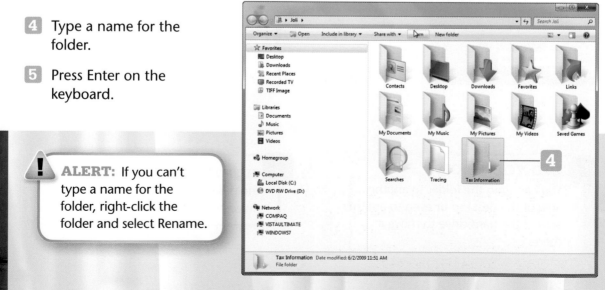

! ALERT: If you can't type a name for the folder, right-click the folder and select Rename.

WHAT DOES THIS MEAN?

Your personal folder contains the following folders, which in turn contain data you've saved:

Contacts: This folder contains your contacts' information, which includes email addresses, pictures, phone numbers, home and business addresses and more.

Desktop: This folder contains links to items for data you created on your desktop.

Downloads: This folder does not contain anything by default. It does offer a place to save items you download from the Internet, like drivers and third-party programs.

Favorites: This folder contains the items in Internet Explorer's Favorites list. It may also include folders created by the computer manufacturer or Microsoft, including Links, Microsoft Websites and MSN Websites.

Links: This folder contains shortcuts to the Documents, Music, Pictures, Public, Recently Changed and Searches folders.

My Documents: This folder contains documents you've saved, subfolders you created and folders created by Windows 7 including Fax, My Received Files, Remote Assistance Logs and Scanned Documents.

My Music: This folder contains sample music and music you save to the PC.

My Pictures: This folder contains sample pictures and pictures you save to the PC.

My Videos: This folder contains sample videos and videos you save to the PC.

Saved Games: This folder contains games that ship with Windows 7 and offers a place to save games you acquire on your own.

Searches: This folder contains preconfigured search folders including Recent Documents, Recent email, Recent Music, Recent Pictures and Videos, Recently Changed and Shared By Me. If you need to find something recently accessed or changed and don't know where to look, you can probably locate it here. These folders get updated each time you open them.

Tracing: Don't worry about this folder, it contains information about your computer.

HOT TIP: When you're ready to save data, you're going to want to save it to the folder that most closely matches the data you're saving. Documents belong in the My Documents folder and pictures belong in the My Pictures folder.

Copy a file

Folders contain files. Files can be documents, pictures, music, videos and more. Sometimes you'll need to copy a file to another location. Perhaps you want to copy the files to an external drive, memory card or USB thumb drive for the purpose of backing it up, or maybe you want to create a copy so you can edit the data in it without worrying about changing the original. You can find files in your personal folders.

1 Locate a file to copy.

2 Right-click the file.

3 While holding down the right mouse key, drag the file to the new location.

4 Drop it there. (It will show Move to Desktop, but once you let go of the mouse you'll have the option to copy or to move.)

5 Choose Copy Here.

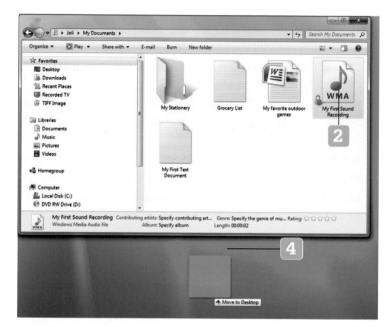

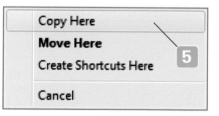

ALERT: To delete the copy, right-click it and choose Delete.

? DID YOU KNOW?

In the example I'm copying a file to the desktop. You can copy files to other folders using the same method, but you'll have to open the folder first (the same applies to moving files).

Move a file

When you copy something, an exact duplicate is made. The original copy of the data remains where it is and a copy of it is placed somewhere else. For the most part, this is not what you want to do when organising data. When organising data, you generally want to move the data. If a picture of a graduation needs to be put in the Graduation Pictures folder, you need to move it, not copy it.

You move a file the same way you copy one, except when you drop the file you choose Move Here instead of Copy Here.

1 Locate a file to move. (See the previous section for more information.)

2 Right-click the file.

3 While holding down the right mouse key, drag the file to the new location.

4 Drop it there.

5 Choose Move Here.

Copy Here
Move Here
Create Shortcuts Here
Cancel

HOT TIP: To put the file back in its original location, repeat these steps dragging the file from the desktop back to the Sample Pictures folder.

HOT TIP: If you don't have any files yet, you can locate a picture file in the Pictures folder. Click Start, click Pictures, and open the Sample Pictures folder (by double-clicking it).

Delete a file

When you are sure you no longer need a particular file, you can delete it. Deleting it sends the file to the Recycle Bin. This file can be 'restored' if you decide you need the file later, provided you have not emptied the Recycle Bin since deleting it.

1 Locate a file to delete.

2 Right-click the file.

3 Choose Delete.

2	

My First Recording

Play
Add to Windows Media Player list
Open With ▶
Share with ▶
Restore previous versions
Send To ▶
Cut
Copy
Create Shortcut
3 — Delete
Rename
Properties

? DID YOU KNOW?

It's best to keep unwanted or unnecessary data off your hard drive. That means you should delete data you don't need, including items in the Recycle Bin.

HOT TIP: In this example I'm deleting a file from the desktop. However, you can also delete files from inside folders, libraries, subfolders and more.

Copy a folder

Folders (and libraries) often contain other folders. Folders contain files including documents, pictures, music, videos and more. Sometimes you'll need to copy a folder to another location. Perhaps you want to copy the folder to an external drive, memory card or USB thumb drive for the purpose of backing it up, or maybe you want to create a copy so you can edit the data in it without worrying about changing the original. You can find folders in your personal folders.

1 Locate a folder to copy.

2 Right-click the folder.

3 While holding down the right mouse key, drag the folder to the new location.

4 Drop it there.

5 Choose Copy Here.

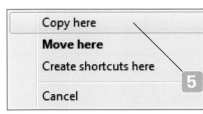

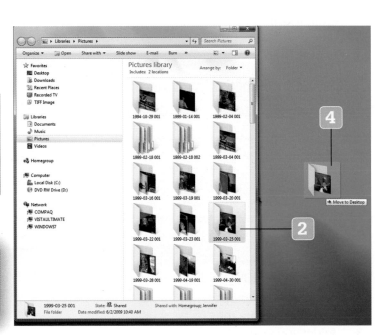

HOT TIP: If you don't have any folders yet, you can copy the Sample Pictures folder.

ALERT: When you copy a folder, you copy all of the data inside it.

DID YOU KNOW?
When you delete a copy of a folder, the original folder remains intact.

Move a folder

When you copy something, an exact duplicate is made. The original copy of the data remains where it is and a copy of it is placed somewhere else. For the most part, this is not what you want to do when organising data. When organising data, you generally want to move the data.

You move a folder the same way you copy one, except when you drop the folder you choose Move here instead of Copy here.

1 Locate a folder to move.

2 Open the folder you want to move it to.

3 Right-click the folder.

4 While holding down the right mouse key, drag the file to the new location.

5 Drop it there.

6 Choose Move here.

6

| Copy here |
| Move here |
| Create shortcuts here |
| Cancel |

? DID YOU KNOW?
You may have to open a folder to locate the folder you want to move.

🔥 HOT TIP: To put the file back in its original location, repeat these steps dragging the file from the desktop back to the original location.

? DID YOU KNOW?
Even though you'll see Copy to <folder name>, when you drop the folder you'll have the option to copy or move the folder.

Delete a folder

When you are sure you no longer need a particular folder, you can delete it. When you delete a folder you delete the folder and everything in it. Deleting it sends the folder and its contents to the Recycle Bin. This folder can be 'restored' if you decide you need it later, provided you have not emptied the Recycle Bin since deleting it.

1 Locate a folder to delete.

2 Right-click the folder.

3 Choose Delete.

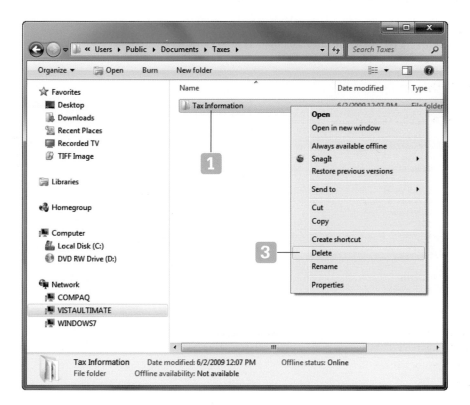

Open a saved file

If you recall, a file can be a document, picture, song, video, presentation, database or other item. You can create documents in Notepad, upload photos from a digital camera, purchase music online and perform other tasks to obtain data. Once data (in this case, a file) is saved to your hard drive, you can access it, open it and often modify it. Most of the time, you open a saved file from a personal folder or a folder you've created.

1 Click Start.

2 Click Documents.

3 Locate the file to open in the Documents folder.

4 Double-click it to open it.

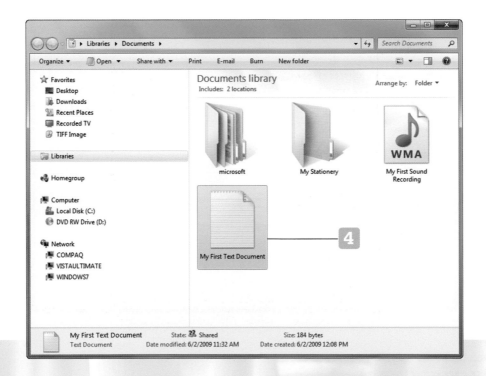

SEE ALSO: Review Write a letter with Notepad and Save a letter with Notepad in Chapter 3 to learn how to create and save a text file.

DID YOU KNOW?
The file will open in the appropriate program automatically.

Search for a file

After you create data, like a Notepad document, you save it to your hard drive. When you're ready to use the file again, you have to locate it and open it. There are several ways to locate a saved file. If you know the document is in the My Documents folder, you can click Start and then click Documents. Then you can simply double-click the file to open it. However, if you aren't sure where the file is, you can search for it from the Start menu.

1 Click Start.

2 In the Start Search window, type the name of the file. If you don't know the exact name of the file, you can type part of the name.

3 Click the file to open it. There will be multiple search results.

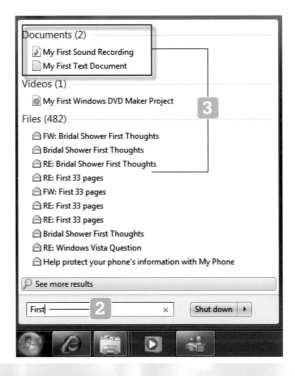

? DID YOU KNOW?

If you don't know any part of the name of the file, you can type a word that is included inside the file or a specific type of file.

Browse for a file

Sometimes you'll open a program, and then open a file associated with it. For instance, you may open Notepad and then open a text file using the File>Open command. After clicking Open, you'll then 'browse' for the file you want. Browsing is the process of locating a file by looking through the available folders on your hard drive from inside an open program.

1 Open Notepad.

2 Click File and click Open.

3 Double-click the file to open. If you do not see the file, proceed to Step 4.

4 In any area in the window, locate the folder that contains the document to open. Double-click the file to open it.

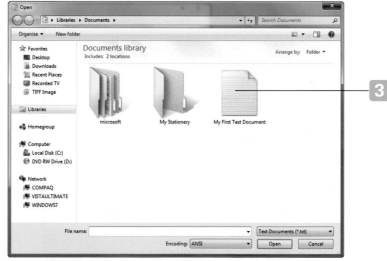

HOT TIP: You can resize the panes too, using the same technique you use to resize a window, by dragging the separator bars.

? DID YOU KNOW?
You can also single-click a file and then click Open.

Explore for a file

Exploring for a file is a bit more complex than the other methods. In this method, you open Windows Explorer and use the Explorer window to locate the file to open.

1 Right-click the Start button and click Open Windows Explorer.

2 Maximise the window and resize the panes to view the contents of the window.

3 In the left pane, expand and collapse folders until you have located the file to open.

4 Double-click the file to open it.

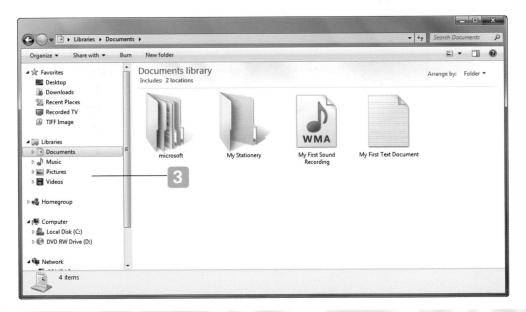

HOT TIP: Libraries let you access specific types of data quickly, no matter where they are stored on the PC.

? DID YOU KNOW?
To expand and collapse any folder, click the arrow next to it.

Back up a folder to an external drive

Once you have your data saved in folders, you can copy the folders to an external drive to create a backup. You copy the folder to the external drive the same way you'd copy a folder to another area of your hard drive – you open both folders and drag and drop.

1 Click Start and click Computer. Position the window so it takes up only about half of the desktop.

2 Locate the external drive. (Leave this window open.)

ALERT: Before you begin, plug in and/or attach the external drive.

SEE ALSO: Restore a window and Move a window in Chapter 2.

3   Locate a folder to copy. If necessary, position the window that contains the folder so you can see both open windows.

4   Right-click the folder to copy.

5   While holding down the right mouse key, drag the folder to the new location.

6   Drop it there.

7   Choose the copy option that is presented. This may be Copy Here or something similar to what's shown below. Don't choose Move Here. This will move the folder off the computer and on to the hard drive.

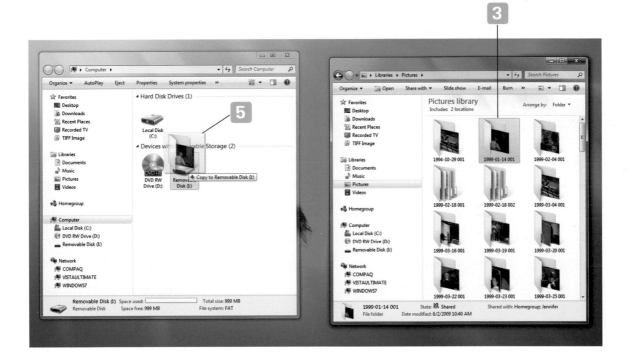

HOT TIP: To locate a folder to copy, click Start and click your personal folder (the one with your name on it).

SEE ALSO: Move a folder earlier in this chapter.

5 Connecting to and surfing the Internet

Introduction

If you aren't online already, now's the time to take the plunge. There are a few things you'll need to do before you can start surfing the Web and emailing friends and family though, like selecting an Internet service provider (ISP), subscribing to it, selecting a user name, password and email address, and obtaining the required configuration settings. Once you have all of that, you'll be ready to go.

There is one exception to subscribing to an ISP and paying for it monthly: you can visit free or minimal cost 'hotspots' where you can get online and with no configuration tasks, provided you have a wireless network adapter installed in your PC. If you have a new laptop, you probably do. If you have a desktop PC, you're probably out of luck. Although you might have a wireless network adapter, you're not going to want to lug your huge PC and a monitor to the local coffee shop just to get online.

Select an ISP

There are a tremendous number of options for connecting to the Internet. You can connect using your phone line (dial-up), using an existing cable connection (broadband or DSL) or wirelessly (satellite). You can also use a connection from a mobile phone provider such as T-Mobile, which is often referred to as mobile broadband. Each of these options offers varying rate plans which are calculated based on how often you go online, whether or not you have an existing service with the provider such as a mobile phone, cable TV, or digital phone, and/or how much 'bandwidth' you use, which has to do with the amount of data you send and receive. This makes choosing an ISP a seemingly daunting task. Making the best choice requires a bit of time and research.

1 Decide where and how you want to access the Internet.
- If you want to connect from anywhere, consider a mobile phone or wireless satellite provider.
- If you want to connect only from home, consider a cable, broadband or DSL.
- If you want to connect for free, find a local hotspot (there's more on this later).

2 Decide whether speed matters to you.
- If you don't travel and speed doesn't matter, consider dial-up. It's inexpensive.
- If you don't travel and speed does matter to you, consider DSL or cable.
- If you travel, you have only one option, satellite. It's not lightning fast, but it is faster than dial-up.

ALERT: If you live 'out in the sticks' where there's no cable TV, you won't be able to get broadband and will have to go with a wireless or dial-up connection.

3 Decide whether cost plays a large role in your decision.

- If cost is an issue, dial-up is the least expensive.
- If you can afford a medium-sized monthly bill, consider cable, broadband or dial-up.
- If you have the money (and need access from anywhere), consider satellite.
- If you can't afford a monthly subscription, consider free Wi-Fi hotspots at your local library or community centre. You'll need a laptop or the ability to use a public computer.

4 Call companies that offer the service you want. Consider your existing mobile phone, cable or satellite TV provider. Many offer bundled pricing.

! ALERT: Don't pay a set-up cost. There are too many companies that will set up your connection for free, making this an unnecessary expense. Note that you may have to purchase hardware though.

🔥 HOT TIP: Decide on a monthly budget. Go to a friend's house if necessary and visit a website such as www.broadband-finder.co.uk to compare prices and services.

Check for a wireless network card

If you have a laptop and don't want to pay for Internet service, you can take your laptop to a 'free Internet hotspot' and connect to the Internet at no cost. However, your laptop must have the required wireless hardware. Specifically, you need a built-in wireless card (or a wireless adapter). You can find out whether you have this hardware using Device Manager.

1 Click Start.

2 In the Start Search dialogue box, type Device Manager.

3 Under Programs, click Device Manager to open it.

4 Locate Network adapters. (Wireless hardware is called network adapters.)

5 Click the plus sign to expand it – it will become a minus sign.

6 Look for a device with the word 'wireless' in it. If you do not see a wireless adapter listed, you do not have wireless capabilities.

7 Click the X in the top right corner of Device Manager to close it.

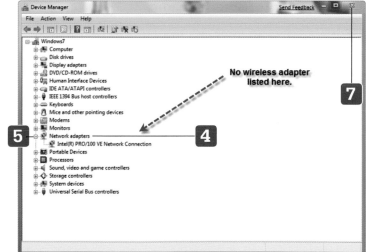

SEE ALSO: Open an application or program, Chapter 1.

? DID YOU KNOW?

Even if you have no adapters, you can purchase a USB converter to obtain satellite Internet or a modem to use dial-up. There's always a way to get online!

Obtain the proper settings

Once you've decided on an ISP, you'll need to call it to set up the subscription. Although you can set up your new account online, you won't get the personal service you deserve. (And you probably don't have a connection to the Internet anyway!) If, after talking to the representative, you are offered a better deal to subscribe online, consider trekking to a friend's house to do it. However, if you explain you don't have access, you may get the better deal anyway. It doesn't hurt to ask.

There are some important things to ask the representative and you must write these things down and keep them in a safe place:

1 User name.

2 Email address.

3 Password.

4 Incoming POP3 server name.

5 Outgoing SMTP server name.

6 Account name (may be the same as user name).

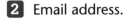 **ALERT:** You'll need this information to set up your email account and to log on to the Internet using your paid service.

HOT TIP: Ask whether the company will be sending you a cable modem, wireless card or wireless modem or other device. Also, ask whether there's an extra fee for someone to come to your home to set it up.

Create a connection

Before you can connect to the Internet, you need to install any hardware you have received. This may mean connecting a cable modem, wireless access point or DSL modem. If you get in a bind, call the ISP. It is there to help. Once the hardware is set up and if the ISP does not walk you through the process of configuring the connection in Windows 7, you'll need to access the Network and Sharing Center to create the connection yourself.

1 Click Start.

2 In the Start Search window, type Network and Sharing.

3 Under Programs, select Network and Sharing Center.

4 Under Tasks, click Set up a new connection or network.

5 Click Connect to the Internet – Set up a wireless, broadband, or dial-up connection to the Internet. Click Next.

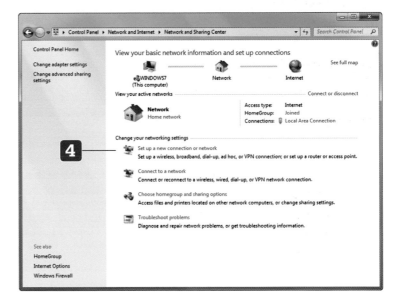

6 When prompted, enter the information you obtained from your Internet service provider. This may include a user name and password.

7 Continue until you've input all of the required information. What you have to input will vary based on your ISP.

> ▶ **SEE ALSO:** Open an application, Chapter 1.

> **?** **DID YOU KNOW?**
> Passwords are case sensitive; user names are usually not.

Diagnose connection problems

If you are having trouble connecting to the Internet through a public or private network, you can diagnose Internet problems using the Network and Sharing Center.

1 Open the Network and Sharing Center.

2 To diagnose a non-working Internet connection, click Troubleshoot problems.

3 Select an option that describes your problem.

4 Work through the troubleshooter to resolve the problem.

? DID YOU KNOW?

There are additional troubleshooting tips in the Help and Support pages. Click Start, and click Help and Support.

! ALERT: If you are connected to the Internet, you will see a green line between your computer and the Internet. If you are not connected you will see a red X.

Join a network

When you connect a new PC running Windows 7 to a wired network or get within range of a wireless one (and you have wireless hardware installed in your computer), Windows 7 will find the network and then ask you what kind of network it is. It's a public network if you're in a coffee shop, library or café, and it's a private network if it's a network you manage, like one already in your home.

1 Connect physically to a wired network using an Ethernet cable or, if you have wireless hardware installed in your laptop, get within range of a wireless network.

2 Select home, work or public location. (If necessary input credentials.)

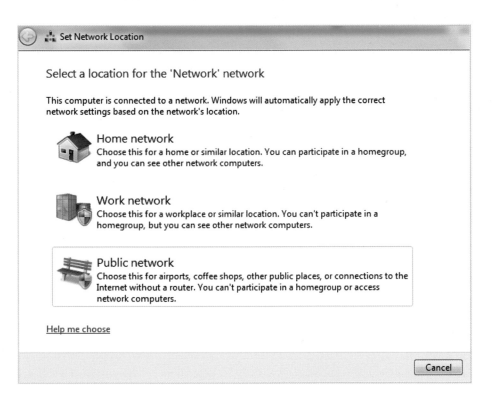

? DID YOU KNOW?

Connecting to an existing network allows you to access shared features of the network. In a coffee shop that will probably be just a connection to the Internet; if it's a home network, it's your personal, shared data (and probably a connection to the Internet too).

🔥 HOT TIP: When a network is accessible, either because you've connected to it using an Ethernet cable or through a wireless network card inside your PC, the Set Network Location wizard will appear.

3 Click the Network icon in the Notification area of the taskbar to determine your connection status.

WHAT DOES THIS MEAN?

There are three network options and when you see the Set Network Location dialogue box, you need to select one. Here's how to know which one to choose:

Home: Choose this if the network is your home network or a network you trust (like a network at a friend's house). This connection type lets your computer *discover* other PCs, printers and devices on the network, and they can see you.

Work: Choose this if you are connecting to a network at work. The settings for Work and Home are the same, only the titles differ so you can tell them apart easily.

Public location: Choose this if the network you want to connect to is open to anyone within range of it, like networks in coffee shops, airports and libraries. Windows 7 figures if you choose Public, you only want to connect to the Internet and nothing else. It closes down *discoverability*, so that even your shared data is safe.

Connect to a free hotspot

Wi-Fi hotspots are popping up all over the country in coffee houses, parks, libraries and more. Wi-Fi hotspots let you connect to the Internet without having to be tethered to an Ethernet cable or tied down with a high monthly wireless bill. You may have to buy a cup of coffee for the privilege, but hey, you were going to anyway, right?

1 Turn on your wireless laptop within range of a free hotspot. You'll be prompted that wireless networks are available.

2 If you see the wireless network you want to connect to in the pop-up, click it. If not, click the network icon in the Notification area of the taskbar to view all of the available wireless networks.

3 Click the network to connect to. You may be connected automatically.

4 If prompted, type the network security key.

5 Click the icon in the Notification area of the taskbar to verify the connection has been made.

Open a website in Internet Explorer

Windows 7 comes with Internet Explorer, an application you can use to surf the Internet. Internet Explorer is a web browser and it has everything you need, including a pop-up blocker, zoom settings, and the ability to save your favourite webpages. You'll use Internet Explorer to surf the Internet.

1 Open Internet Explorer from the taskbar. It's a big, blue E. A website will probably open automatically.

2 To go to a website you want to visit, type the name of the website in the window at the top of the page. This is called the address bar.

3 Press Enter on the keyboard.

HOT TIP: You can also drag your mouse across an open website name to select it. Do not drag your mouse over the http://www part of the address and you won't have to retype it.

WHAT DOES THIS MEAN?

Address bar: Used to type in Internet addresses, also known as URLs (uniform resource locators). Generally, an Internet address takes the form of http://www.*companyname*.com.

Open a website in a new tab

You can open more than one website at a time in Internet Explorer. To do this, click the tab that appears to the right of the open webpage. Then type the name of the web site you'd like to visit.

1 Open Internet Explorer.

2 Click an empty tab.

3 Type the name of the website you'd like to visit in the address bar.

4 Press Enter on the keyboard.

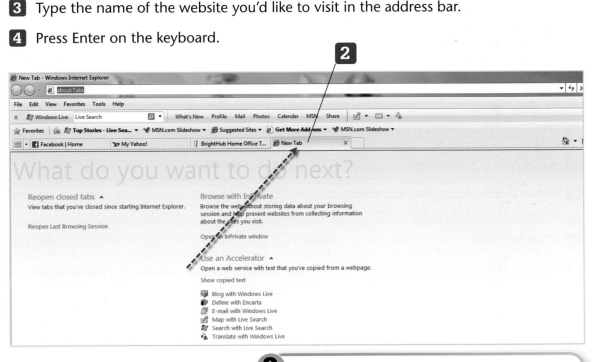

ALERT: Web sites almost always start with http://www.

? DID YOU KNOW?
When a website name starts with https://, it means it's secure. When purchasing items online, make sure the payment pages have this prefix.

WHAT DOES THIS MEAN?

The Internet Explorer interface has several distinct parts:

Command bar: Used to access icons such as the Home and Print icons.

Tabs: Used to access websites when multiple sites are open.

Search window: Used to search for anything on the Internet.

Set a home page

You can select a single webpage or multiple webpages to be displayed each time you open Internet Explorer. In fact, there are three options for configuring home pages:

- Use this webpage as your only home page – select this option if you only want one page to serve as your home page.
- Add this webpage to your home pages tabs – select this option if you want this page to be one of several home pages.
- Use the current tab set as your home page – select this option if you've opened multiple tabs and you want all of them to be home pages.

1 Use the address bar to locate a webpage you want to use as your home page.

2 Click the arrow next to the Home icon.

3 Click Add or Change Home Page.

4 Make a selection using the information provided regarding each option.

5 Click Yes.

6 Repeat these steps as desired.

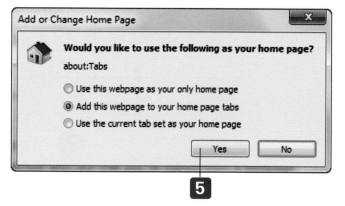

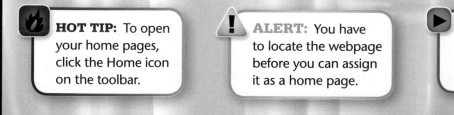

HOT TIP: To open your home pages, click the Home icon on the toolbar.

ALERT: You have to locate the webpage before you can assign it as a home page.

SEE ALSO: Open a website in Internet Explorer, earlier in this chapter.

Mark a favourite

Favourites are websites you save links to for accessing more easily at a later time. They differ from home pages because by default they do not open when you start Internet Explorer. The favourites you save appear in the Favourites Center and on the Favorites bar. You may see some favourites listed that you did not create, including Microsoft and MSN websites. Every time you save a favourite, it will appear in both places.

1 Go to the webpage you want to configure as a favourite.

2 Click the Add to Favourites icon.

3 Note the new icon for the favourite on the Favourites bar.

4 Click the Favorites icon. The Favourites Center opens.

5 Click the folders to view the favorites listed in them.

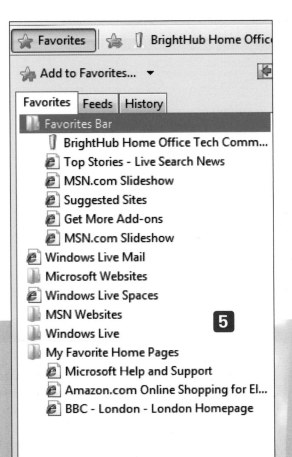

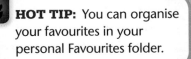

HOT TIP: You can organise your favourites in your personal Favourites folder.

Change the zoom level of a webpage

If you have trouble reading what's on a webpage because the text is too small, use the Page Zoom feature. Page Zoom preserves the fundamental design of the webpage you're viewing. This means that Page Zoom intelligently zooms in on the entire page, which maintains the page's integrity, layout and look.

1 Open Internet Explorer and browse to a webpage.

2 Click the arrow located at the bottom right of Internet Explorer to show the Zoom options.

3 Click 150%.

4 Notice how the webpage text and images increase. Use the scroll bars to navigate the page.

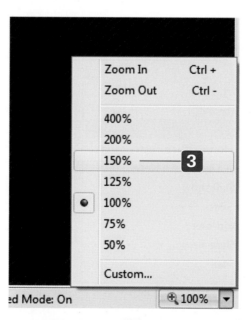

? DID YOU KNOW?

The term browse is used to describe both locating a file on your hard drive and locating something on the Internet.

? DID YOU KNOW?

The Page Zoom options are located under the Page icon on the Command bar, under Zoom, but it's much easier to use the link at the bottom right of the browser window, on the Status bar.

Print a webpage

To print a webpage, simply click the Print icon on the Command bar.

1 Open Internet Explorer and browse to a webpage.

2 Click the Print icon to print the page with no further input.

3 To view print options, click the arrow next to the Print icon.

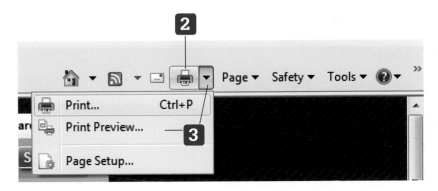

? DID YOU KNOW?

You can use the Snipping Tool (Chapter 3) to take a screen shot of a webpage and then you can write notes on it, email it or save it.

WHAT DOES THIS MEAN?

There are three menu options under the Print icon:

Print: Clicking Print opens the Print dialogue box where you can configure the page range, select a printer, change page orientation, change print order and choose a paper type. Additional options include print quality, output bins and more. Of course, the choices depend on what your printer offers. If your printer can print only at 300×300 dots per inch, you can't configure it to print at a higher quality.

Print Preview: Clicking Print Preview opens a window where you can see before you print what the printout will actually look like. You can switch between portrait and landscape views, access the Page Setup dialogue box, and more.

Page Setup: Clicking Page Setup opens the Page Setup dialogue box. Here you can select a paper size, source, and create headers and footers. You can also change orientation and margins, all of which is dependent on what features your printer supports.

Clear history

If you don't want people to be able to snoop around on your computer and find out what sites you've been visiting you'll need to delete your 'browsing history'. Deleting your browsing history lets you remove the information stored on your computer related to your Internet activities.

1 Open Internet Explorer.

2 Click the Alt key on the keyboard if you do not see the menu shown here.

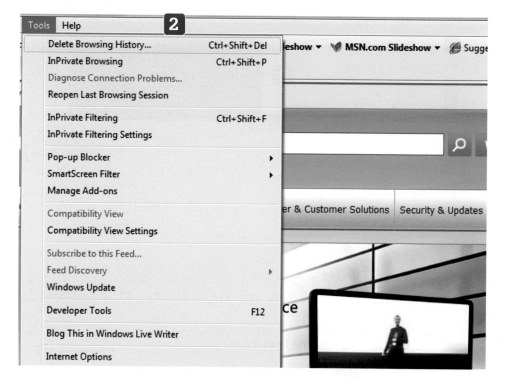

ALERT: Clicking the Alt key on the keyboard is what causes the Menu bar to appear.

DID YOU KNOW?
You can also click Safety and then Delete Browsing History.

3 Click Tools.

4 Click Delete Browsing History.

5 To delete any or all of the listed items, click the Delete button.

6 Click Close when finished.

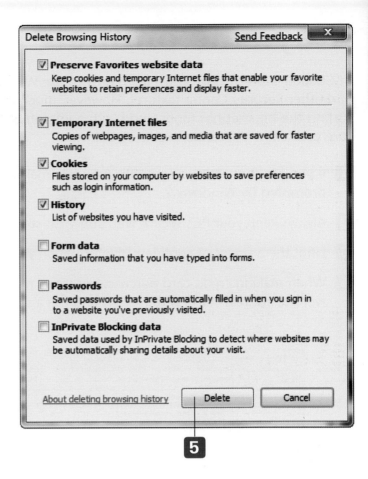

5

WHAT DOES THIS MEAN?

Temporary Internet Files: Files that have been downloaded and saved in your Temporary Internet Files folder. A snooper could go through these files to see what you've been doing online.

Cookies: Small text files that include data that identifies your preferences when you visit particular websites. Cookies are what allow you to visit, say, www.amazon.com and be greeted with 'Hello <your name>, We have recommendations for you!' Cookies help a site offer you a personalised web experience.

History: The list of websites you've visited and any web addresses you've typed. Anyone can look at your History list to see where you've been.

Form data: Information that's been saved using Internet Explorer's autocomplete form data functionality. If you don't want forms to be filled out automatically by you or someone else who has access to your PC and user account, delete this.

Passwords: Passwords that were saved using Internet Explorer autocomplete password prompts.

InPrivate Blocking data: Data that was saved by InPrivate Blocking to detect where websites may be automatically sharing details about your visit.

Stay safe online

In Chapter 7 on security you'll learn how to use Windows Firewall, Windows Defender and other Security Center features. However, much of staying secure when online and surfing the Internet has more to do with common sense. When you're online, make sure you follow the guidelines listed below.

1 If you are connecting to a public network, make sure you select Public when prompted by Windows 7.

2 Always keep your PCs secure with anti-virus software.

3 Limit the amount of confidential information you store on the Internet.

4 When making credit card purchases or travel reservations, always make sure the website address starts with https:// and use a secure site.

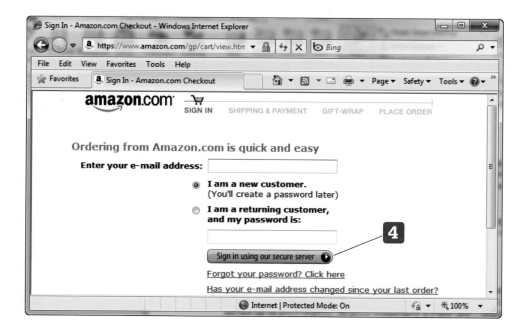

? DID YOU KNOW?
When you connect to a network you know, like a network in your home, you select Home (or Work).

! ALERT: You have to purchase and install your own anti-virus software; it does not come with Windows 7.

5 Always sign out of any secure website you enter.

Joli Ballew | Edit Profile | Writer Dashboard | Sign out

SEARCH

WHAT DOES THIS MEAN?

Domain Name: For our use here, a domain name is synonymous with a website name.

Favorite: A webpage that you've chosen to maintain a shortcut for in the Favorites Center.

Home page: The webpage that opens when you open IE7. You can set the home page and configure additional pages to open as well.

Link: A shortcut to a webpage. Links are often offered in an email, document or webpage to allow you to access a site without having to actually type in its name. In almost all instances, links are underlined and in a different colour than the page they are configured on.

Load: A webpage must 'load' before you can access it. Some pages load instantly while others take a few seconds.

Navigate: The process of moving from one webpage to another or viewing items on a single webpage. Often the term is used as follows: 'Click the link to navigate to the new web page'.

Search: A term used when you type a word or group of words into a Search window. Searching for data produces results.

Scroll up and scroll down: The process of using the scroll bars on a webpage or the arrow keys on a keyboard to move up and down the pages of a website.

Website: A group of webpages that contains related information. Microsoft's website contains information about Microsoft products, for instance.

URL: The information you type to access a website, such as http://www.microsoft.com.

ALERT: Don't put your address and phone number on Facebook or other social networking sites.

HOT TIP: The 's' after http lets you know it's a secure site.

6 Working with email

Introduction

Previous versions of Windows operating systems, like Windows XP and Windows Vista, came with an email program built in. That's not the case with Windows 7. However, Microsoft does offer Windows Live Mail, which you can download and install for free on your Windows 7 PC. Windows Live Mail lets you access your email from any PC that has Internet access, not just the PC in your home or office.

Windows Live Mail is the only thing you need to view, send and receive email, manage your contacts and manage sent, saved and incoming email. Within Windows Live Mail you can also print email, create folders for storing email you want to keep, manage unwanted email, open attachments, send pictures inside an email and more.

To use Windows Live Mail (after installation), you need an email address and two email server addresses, all of which you can get from your ISP. In fact, you probably have this information if you worked through Chapter 5, Connecting to and surfing the Internet. With this information in hand, you'll work through the simple wizard boxes, inputting the required information when prompted, to set up the program. Once Mail is set up, you're ready to send and receive mail. Don't worry, it's easy!

Download and install Windows Live Mail

If you've never downloaded and/or installed a program before, you may be a little nervous about doing so. Don't worry, it's really easy, and Microsoft has set it up so that the process requires very little input from you. There are only a few steps: go to the website, click the Download link and wait for the download and installation process to complete.

1 Open Internet Explorer and go to http://www.windowslive.com/mail.

2 Look for the Download now button and click it. You'll be prompted to click Download now once more on the next screen.

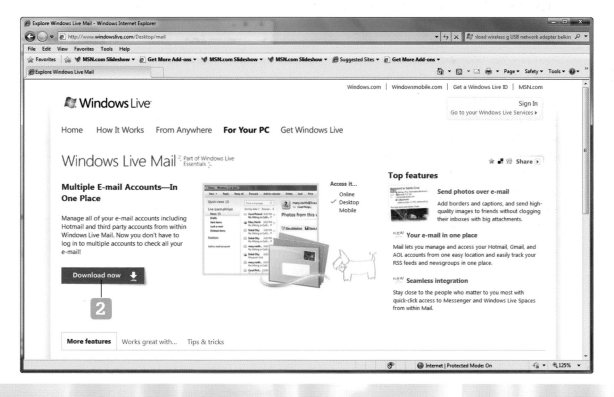

3 Click Run and when prompted, click Yes.

4 When prompted, select the items to download. You can select all of the items some of the items or only Mail. Then click Install.

5 When prompted to select your settings, make the desired choices. You can't go wrong here; there are no bad options.

HOT TIP: Select Mail, Photo Gallery and Toolbar, for best results. We'll be covering these programs in this book.

? DID YOU KNOW?
It's OK to select all of these programs if you think you'll use them – they are all free.

Get a Windows Live account

When you use 'Live' services, like Windows Live Mail, Windows Live Photo Gallery and others, you have to log in to them using a Windows Live account. A Windows Live account is an email address and password you use to log on to your Live programs on the Internet. This account is free and you can use it to sign in to all Live-related websites.

1 If you do not already have a Windows Live account, click Sign up after the installation of Live Mail completes. (You can also go to https://signup.live.com.)

2 Fill out the required information and click I accept when finished.

Windows Live

Welcome to Windows Live!

Your new programs are in the Windows Live folder on the Start menu.

Do you have a Windows Live ID?
To get the most from your new programs, use your Windows Live ID to sign in.
If you use Hotmail, Messenger, or Xbox LIVE, you already have a Windows Live ID. If not, it only takes a minute to sign up.

Sign up

1

Close

Create your Windows Live ID
It gets you into all Windows Live services—and other places you see
All information is required.

ⓘ Already using **Hotmail**, **Messenger**, or **Xbox LIVE**? Sign in now

Use your e-mail address: *Example: someone@example.com*
Or get a Windows Live e-mail address
Create a password:
6-character minimum; case sensitive
Retype password:
First name:
Last name:
Country/region: United States ▼
State: Select one ▼
ZIP code:
Gender: ⚪ Male ⚪ Female
Birth year: *Example: 1990*

B9VP9NE6

Characters:
Enter the 8 characters you see

2

? DID YOU KNOW?
You can use your Windows Live email account as a regular email address, or simply use it to log into Live services on the Internet.

🔥 HOT TIP: Fill out the information with true information. This is an ID, after all.

Set up the Windows Live email account in Mail

The first time you open Windows Live Mail you'll be prompted to input the required information regarding your email address and email servers. That's because Windows Live Mail is a program for sending and receiving email and you can't do that without inputting the proper information. The easiest email account to set up is the one configured in the previous section, Get a Windows Live account. That's what you'll do here.

1 Open Windows Live Mail.

2 If you are not prompted to add e-mail account information, click Add e-mail account.

3 Type your Windows Live email account, password and display name.

4 If desired, leave Remember password ticked. Click Next.

5 Click Finish, and if prompted, click Download Now to retrieve your email. (Don't tick Manually configure server settings for email account.)

Add e-mail account

2

Add an E-mail Account

Please enter your e-mail account information below:

3 E-mail address: Joli_Ballew@hotmail.com
example555@hotmail.com   Get a free e-mail account
Password: ••••••••
☑ Remember password   **4**
How should your name appear in e-mail sent from this account?
Display Name: Joli Ballew
For example: John Smith

☐ Manually configure server settings for e-mail account.

Next   Cancel

? DID YOU KNOW?

Your email address often takes this form: *yourname@yourispname.com*. Your Display name can be anything you like.

? DID YOU KNOW?

Your Display name is the name that will appear in the From field when you compose an email and in the sender's Inbox (under From in their email list) when people receive email from you.

Set up a third-party email account

When you set up a Windows Live email account, Windows Live knows what settings to use and configure in the background. If you want to set up a third-party email account, you have to enter the settings manually. You get the information you need from your ISP.

1 Open Mail and click Add e-mail account.

2 Input your email address, password and display name as detailed in the previous section.

3 When prompted, fill in the information for your incoming and outgoing mail servers. You must input exactly what your ISP tells you to input! When in doubt, call the ISP or check its website for the proper settings. Click Next.

4 Click Finish.

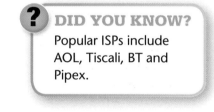

? DID YOU KNOW?
Popular ISPs include AOL, Tiscali, BT and Pipex.

! ALERT: If your ISP told you your outgoing server requires authentication, tick the box. If you aren't sure, don't tick it.

! ALERT: To resolve errors, click Tools, click Accounts, click the email account to change and click Properties. You can then make changes to the mail servers, passwords and other settings.

View an email

Windows Live Mail checks for email automatically when you first open the program and every 30 minutes thereafter. If you want to check for email manually, you can click the Sync button any time you want. When you receive mail, there are two ways to read it. You can click the message once and read it in the Mail window, or double-click it to open it in its own window. I think it's best to simply click the email once, that way you don't have multiple open windows to deal with.

1 Click the Sync button.

2 Click the email once.

3 View the contents of the email.

ALERT: Email is received in the Inbox or the Unread e-mail box. If one of these is not selected, you must select it first!

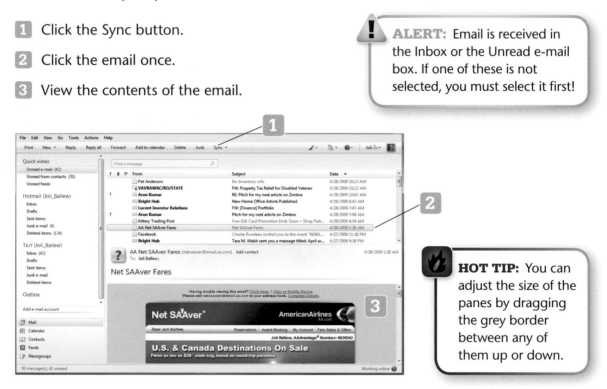

HOT TIP: You can adjust the size of the panes by dragging the grey border between any of them up or down.

WHAT DOES THIS MEAN?

Inbox: This folder holds mail you've received.

Outbox: This folder holds mail you've written but have not yet sent.

Sent Items: This folder stores copies of messages you've sent.

Deleted Items: This folder holds mail you've deleted.

Drafts: This folder holds messages you've started and saved but not completed. Click File and click Save to put an email in progress here.

Junk e-mail: This folder holds email that Windows Live Mail thinks is spam. You should check this folder occasionally, since Mail may put email in there you want to read.

Unread e-mail: This folder shows email you have yet to read. Note there is one that contains email from contacts too. The latter shows only email from contacts in your address book.

Change how often Mail checks for email

You may want Mail to check for email more or less often than every 30 minutes. It's easy to make the change.

1 Click Tools. (If you can't see the Tools menu, press the Alt key on the keyboard.)

2 Click Options.

3 Click the General tab.

4 Change the number of minutes from 30 to something else.

5 Click OK.

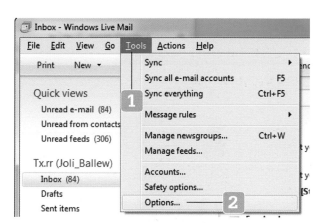

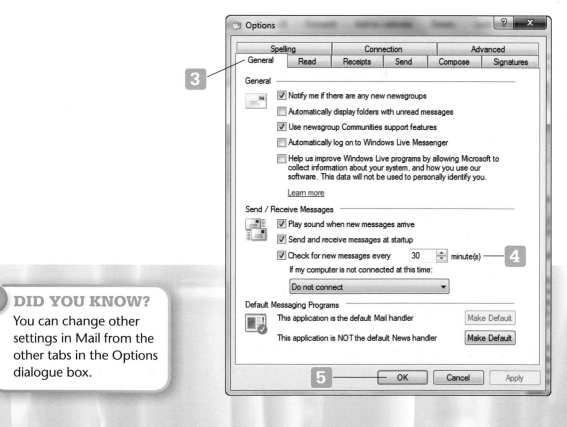

? DID YOU KNOW?

You can change other settings in Mail from the other tabs in the Options dialogue box.

View an attachment

An attachment is a file that you can send with an email, such as a picture, document or video clip. If an email you receive contains an attachment, you'll see a paperclip. To open the attachment, click the paperclip icon in the Preview pane and click the attachment's name.

1 Locate the paperclip icon in the Message pane and click it once.

2 Click Open.

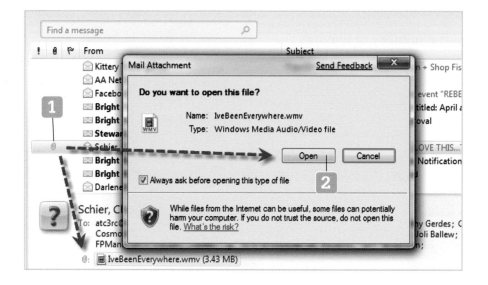

ALERT: Hackers send attachments that look like they are from legitimate companies, banks and online services. Do not open these. Companies rarely send email attachments.

ALERT: Attachments can contain viruses. Never open an attachment from someone you don't know.

HOT TIP: Never open an attachment that ends in .zip unless you are sure it is from someone you trust and that it is not a virus.

Recover email from the Junk e-mail folder

Windows Live Mail has a junk email filter and anything it thinks is spam gets sent there. (Spam is another word for junk email.) Unfortunately, sometimes email that is actually legitimate email gets sent to the Junk e-mail folder. Therefore, once a week or so you should look in this folder to see whether any email you want to keep is in there.

1 Click the Junk e-mail folder one time.

2 Use the scroll bars if necessary to browse through the email in the folder.

3 If you see an email that is legitimate, click it once.

4 Click Not junk.

5 Click Inbox to view the e-mail.

HOT TIP: When you click Not junk, the email is sent to your Inbox.

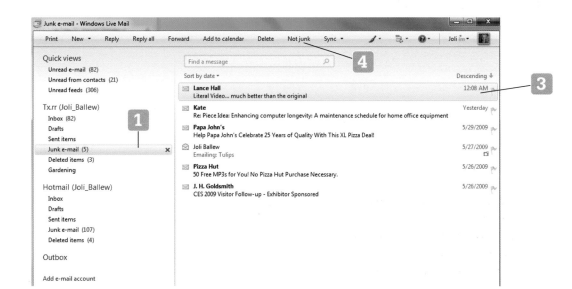

HOT TIP: When you tell Mail that a certain email is 'not junk', it remembers and should not flag email from this sender as spam again.

ALERT: Mail requires routine maintenance, including deleting email from the Junk e-mail folder, among other things. You'll learn how to delete items in a folder later in this chapter.

Reply to an email

When someone sends you an email, you may need to send a reply to them. You do that by selecting the email and then clicking the Reply button.

1 Select the email you want to reply to in the Message pane.

2 Click Reply.

3 Type the message in the body pane.

4 Click Send.

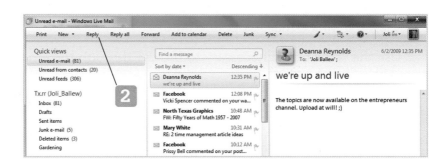

Forward an email

When someone sends you an email that you want to share with others, you forward the email. You do that by selecting the email and then clicking the Forward button.

1 Select the email you want to forward in the Message pane.

2 Click Forward.

3 In the To: field, type the email address for the recipient.

4 Type a subject in the Subject field.

5 Type the message in the body pane.

6 Click Send.

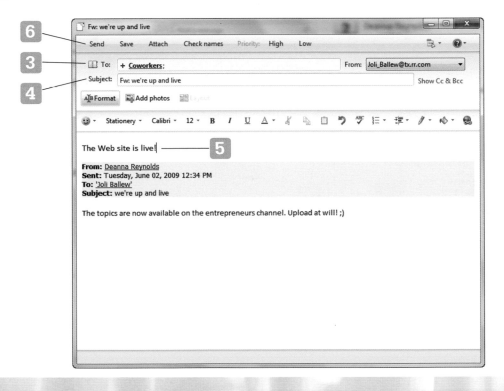

DID YOU KNOW?
Forwarded email contains FW: in the subject line by default.

DID YOU KNOW?
People often forward funny jokes.

Compose and send an email

You compose an email message by clicking New on the toolbar. You input who the email should be sent to and the subject, and then you type the message.

1 Click New.

2 Type the recipient's email address in the To: line. If you want to add additional names, separate each email address by a semicolon.

3 Type a subject in the Subject field.

4 Type the message in the body pane.

5 Click Send.

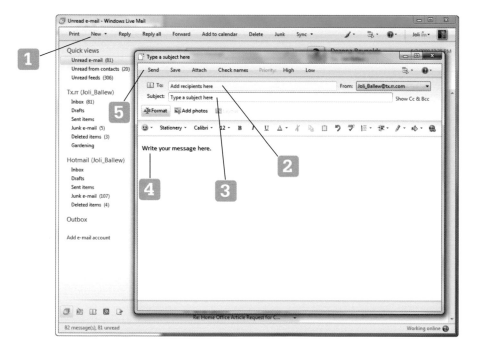

HOT TIP: Make sure the subject adequately describes the body of your email. Your recipients should be able to review the subject line later and recall what the email was regarding.

WHAT DOES THIS MEAN?

CC: Stands for carbon copy.
Bcc: Stands for blind carbon copy and is a secret copy.

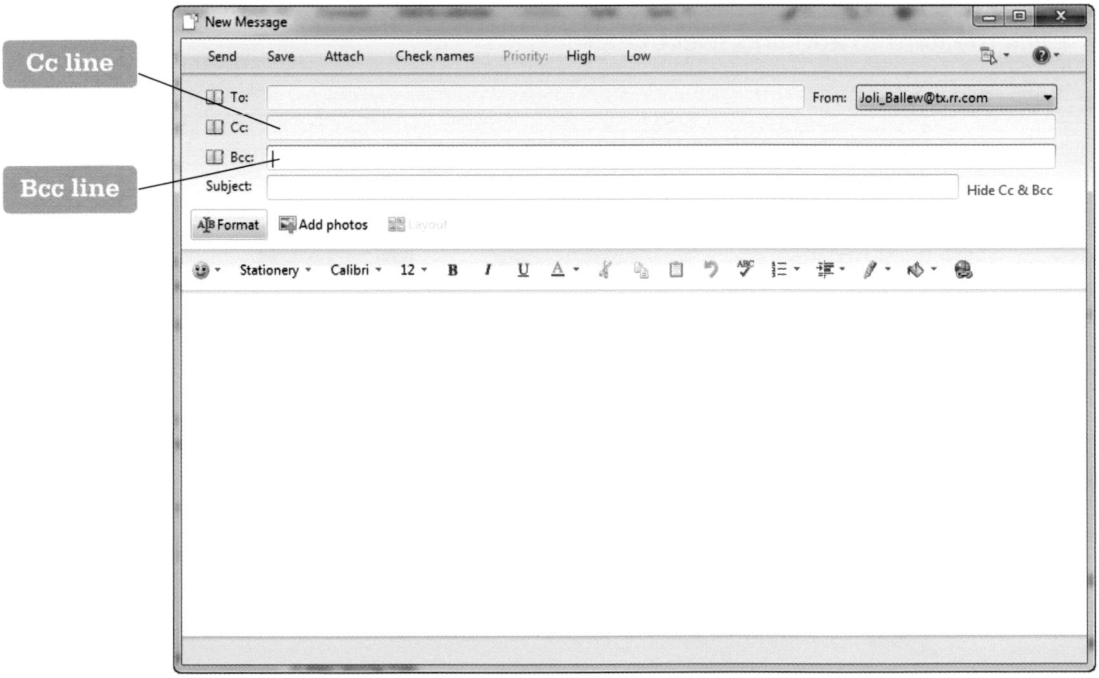

Cc line

Bcc line

New Message
Send Save Attach Check names Priority: High Low
To:	From: Joli_Ballew@tx.rr.com
Cc:
Bcc:
Subject:	Hide Cc & Bcc
Format Add photos Layout
Stationery ▾ Calibri ▾ 12 ▾ B I U A ▾

HOT TIP: Select Tools and click Select from contacts to add email addresses from your address book.

Attach a picture to an email using Insert

Although email that contains only a message serves its purpose quite a bit of the time, often you'll want to send a photograph, a short video, a sound recording, a document or other data. When you want to add something to your message other than text, it's called adding an attachment. There are many ways to attach something to an email. One way is to use the Insert menu and choose File as attachment. Then you can browse to the location of the attachment and click Insert.

1 Click New to create a new mail message.

2 Click Attach.

3 Locate the file to attach.

4 Click the item to add and select Open.

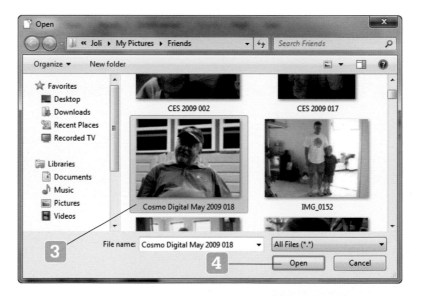

HOT TIP: When inserting (adding) files to an email, hold down the Ctrl key to select non-contiguous files or the Shift key to select contiguous ones.

ALERT: Anything you attach won't be removed from your computer; instead, a copy will be created for the attachment.

Attach a picture to an email using a right-click

You can create an email that contains an attachment by right-clicking the file you want to attach. This method attaches the files to a new email, which is fine if you want to create a new email. The only problem with this is that it doesn't work if you'd rather send forwards or replies. However, this method has a feature other methods don't. With this method, you can resize any images you've selected before sending them. This is a great perk because many pictures are too large to send via email and resizing them helps manage an email's size.

1 Locate the file you'd like to attach and right-click it.

2 Point to Send to.

3 Click Mail recipient.

? DID YOU KNOW?

You can email from within applications, such as Microsoft Word or Excel. Generally, you'll find the desired option under the File menu, as a submenu of Send.

! ALERT: Avoid sending large attachments, especially to people you know have a dial-up modem or those who get email only on a small device like a BlackBerry, iPhone or Mobile PC.

4 If the item you're attaching is a picture, choose the picture size. Click Attack.

5 Click Yes to turn the message into a photo email and the recipient will be able to view the picture in a slideshow using Windows Live on the Internet. (Try it and see!)

6 Complete the email and click Send.

Attach Files

Picture size: Medium: 1024 x 768   **4**

Total estimated size: 230 KB

Attach   Cancel

4

Photo E-Mail

Turn this message into a photo e-mail?

With photo e-mail, you upload high-resolution photos to the Web but send small thumbnails in your message. Recipients receive smaller messages and view your photos in an online slideshow. They can also download the high-resolutions photos that they want.

☐ Don't ask me this again.

5   Yes   No

? **DID YOU KNOW?**

800 × 600 is usually the best option when sending pictures via email.

Add a contact

A contact is a data file that holds the information you keep about a person. The contact information looks like a 'contact card' and the information can include a picture, email address, mailing address, first and last name and similar data. You obtain contacts from various sources: people you email, people you instant message with Windows Live Messenger and more.

1 From Windows Live Mail, click Contacts.

2 Click New.

3 Type all of the information you wish to add. Be sure to add information to each tab.

4 Click Add contact.

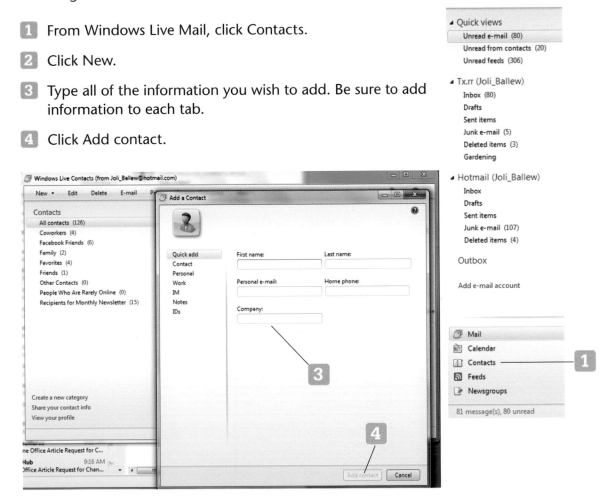

◢ Quick views
    Unread e-mail (80)
    Unread from contacts (20)
    Unread feeds (306)

◢ Tx.rr (Joli_Ballew)
    Inbox (80)
    Drafts
    Sent items
    Junk e-mail (5)
    Deleted items (3)
    Gardening

◢ Hotmail (Joli_Ballew)
    Inbox
    Drafts
    Sent items
    Junk e-mail (107)
    Deleted items (4)

    Outbox

    Add e-mail account

Mail
Calendar
Contacts
Feeds
Newsgroups

81 message(s), 80 unread

? DID YOU KNOW?

When someone gives you their email address and other personal data, you can create a contact card for them. From the File menu, select New, then select Contact.

HOT TIP: Your contacts are stored in your Contacts folder inside your personal folder.

Print an email

Sometimes you'll need to print an email or its attachment. Windows Live Mail makes it easy to print – just click Print on the toolbar. After clicking Print, the Print dialogue box will appear where you can select a printer, set print preferences, choose a page range and, well, print. If you don't see a Print icon, press the Alt key on the keyboard, click File and then click Print.

1 Select the email to print by clicking it in the Message pane.

2 If neccessary, click Alt on the keyboard to show the Menu bar. Then click File and Print.

3 In the Print dialogue box, select the printer to use if more than one exists.

4 Click Print.

You can configure print preferences and choose what pages to print using Preferences. Refer to your printer's user manual to find out what print options your printer supports.

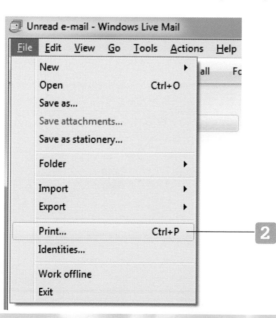

Apply a junk mail filter

Just like you receive unwanted information from phone solicitors, radio stations and television ads, you're going to get unwanted advertisements in emails. This is referred to as junk email or spam. Most of these advertisements are scams and rip-offs and they also often contain pornographic images. There are four filtering options in Windows Live Mail: No Automatic Filtering, Low, High and Safe List Only.

1 Click the Menus icon and click Safety options.

2 From the Options tab, make a selection.

3 Click the Phishing tab.

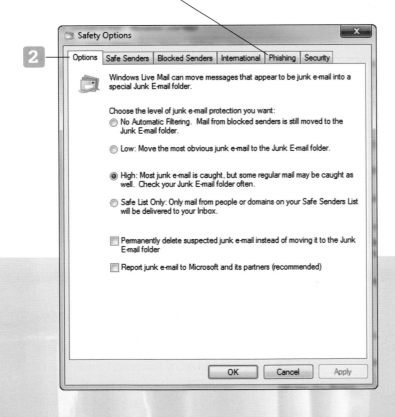

? DID YOU KNOW?
Click the Alt key on the keyboard and click Tools, then Safety options.

4 Select Protect my Inbox from messages with potential Phishing links. Additionally, move phishing email to the Junk E-Mail folder.

5 Click OK.

▶ **SEE ALSO:** Recover email from the Junk e-mail folder, earlier in this chapter.

WHAT DOES THIS MEAN?

No Automatic Filtering: Use this only if you do not want Windows Live Mail to block junk email messages. Windows Live Mail will continue to block messages from email addresses listed on the Blocked Senders list.

Low: Use this option if you receive very little junk email. You can start here and increase the filter if it becomes necessary.

High: Use this option if you receive a lot of junk email and want to block as much of it as possible. Use this option for children's email accounts. Note that some valid email will probably be blocked, so you'll have to review the Junk e-mail folder occasionally, to make sure you aren't missing any email you want to keep.

Safe List Only: Use this option if you only want to receive messages from people or domain names on your Safe Senders list. This is a drastic step and requires you to add every sender you want to receive mail from to the Safe Senders list. Use this as a last resort.

⚠ **ALERT:** Never buy anything from a junk email, send money to a sick or dying stranger, send money for your portion of a lottery ticket or fall for other spam hoaxes.

⚠ **ALERT:** Don't give your email address to any website or company, or include it in any registration card, unless you're willing to receive junk email from them and their constituents.

Create a folder

It's important to perform some housekeeping chores once a month or so. If you don't, Windows Live Mail may bog down and perform more slowly than it should, or you may be unable to manage the email you want to keep. One way you can keep Mail under control is to create a new folder to hold email you want to keep and move mail into it.

1 Click the arrow next to New and click Folder.

2 Type a name for the new folder.

3 Select any folder (e.g. Inbox). The folder you create will appear underneath it.

4 Click OK.

New ▾	Reply	Reply all	Fo
E-mail message		Ctrl+N	
Photo e-mail		Ctrl+Shift+P	
Event		Ctrl+Shift+E	
News message		Ctrl+Shift+W	
Contact		Ctrl+Shift+N	
Folder		Ctrl+Shift+D	

Create Folder

Folder name:

Funny Jokes

OK

Cancel

Select the folder in which to create the new folder:

Tx.rr (Joli_Ballew)
  Inbox
  Drafts
  Sent items
  Junk e-mail
  Deleted items
  Gardening

Hotmail (Joli_Ballew)
  Inbox
  Drafts
  Sent items

🔥 **HOT TIP:** Name folders descriptively, for instance Funny Jokes, Receipts or Pictures.

❓ **DID YOU KNOW?**
Using the same technique, you can create subfolders inside folders you create.

Move email to a folder

Moving an email from one folder (like your Inbox) to another (like Funny Jokes) is a simple task. Just drag the email from one folder to the other.

1 Right-click the email message to move in the Message pane.

2 Hold down the mouse button while dragging the message to the new folder.

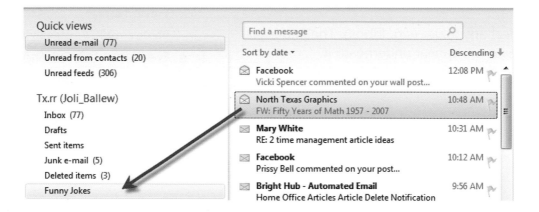

HOT TIP: To access the email again, click the folder. The emails in that folder will appear in the Message pane.

Delete email in a folder

In order to keep Mail from getting bogged down, you'll need to delete email in folders often. Depending on how much email you get, this may be as often as once a week.

1 Right-click Junk e-mail.

2 Click Empty 'Junk e-mail' folder.

3 Right-click Deleted items.

4 Click Empty 'Deleted items' folder.

▲ Hotmail (Joli_Ballew)
   Inbox
   Drafts
   Sent items
   Junk e-mail (107)
   Deleted items (4)

Outbox

Add e-mail account

   Mail
   Calendar
   Contacts
   Feeds
   Newsgroups

165 message(s), 107 unread

Fw: FW: Why Aspirin by your bed?

☒ **adams ali**
READ AND GET BACK TO ME

☒ **^Samp1ePackz^**
C1AL1S 0r V1AGRA FOR FR33

| Open |
| Empty 'Junk e-mail' folder |
| Find... |
| Mark all as read   Ctrl+Shift+A |
| New folder... |
| Rename... |
| Delete |
| Synchronization settings   ▶ |
| Add to compact view |
| Set color   ▶ |
| Properties |

HOT TIP: Select any email in any folder and click the red X to delete it.

ALERT: Don't forget to empty your Sent items folders occasionally too.

7 Stay secure

Introduction

Windows 7 comes with a lot of built-in features to keep you and your data safe. Windows 7 security tools and features help you avoid email scams, harmful websites and hackers, and also help you protect your data and your computer from unscrupulous co-workers or nosy family members. If you know how to take advantage of the available safeguards, you'll be protected in almost all cases. You just need to be aware of the dangers, heed security warnings when they are given (and resolve them) and use all of the available features in Windows 7 to protect yourself and your PC.

Add a new user account

You created your user account when you first turned on your new Windows 7 PC. Your user account is what defines your personal folders as well as your settings for desktop background, screen saver and other items. You are the 'administrator' of your computer. If you share the PC with someone, they should have their own user account. If every person who accesses your PC has their own standard user account and password, and if every person logs on using that account and then logs off the PC each time they've finished using it, you'll never have to worry about anyone accessing anyone else's personal data.

1 Click Start.

2 Click Control Panel.

3 Click Add or remove user accounts.

4 Click Create a new account.

5 Type a new account name, verify Standard user is selected and click Create Account. You can click Change the picture, Change the account name, Remove the password and other options to further personalise the account.

? DID YOU KNOW?

Administrators can make changes to system-wide settings but standard users cannot (without an administrator name and password).

! ALERT: All accounts should have a password applied to them. Refer to the next section, Require a password.

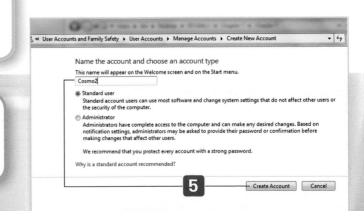

Require a password

All user accounts, even yours, should be password-protected. When a password is configured, you must type the password to log on to your PC or laptop. This protects the PC from unauthorised access.

1 Click Start.

2 Click Control Panel.

3 Click Add or remove user accounts.

4 Click the user account to apply a password to.

5 Click Create a password.

6 Type the new password, type it again to confirm it and type a password hint.

7 Click Create password.

ALERT: Create a password that contains upper- and lower-case letters and a few numbers. Write the password down and keep it somewhere out of sight and safe.

? DID YOU KNOW?

When you need to make a system-wide change, you have to be logged on as an administrator or type an administrator's user name and password.

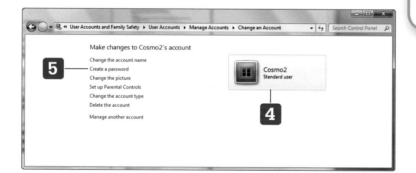

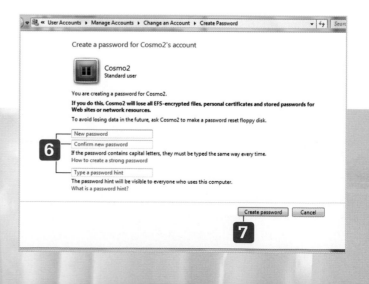

Configure Windows Update

It's very important to configure Windows Update to get and install updates automatically. This is the easiest way to ensure your computer is as up to date as possible, at least as far as patching security flaws Microsoft uncovers, having access to the latest features and obtaining updates to the operating system itself. I propose you verify that the recommended settings are enabled as detailed here and occasionally check for optional updates manually.

1 Click Start.

2 Click Control Panel.

3 Click System and Security.

4 Click Windows Update.

5 In the left pane, click Change settings.

Adjust your computer's settings

System and Security **3**
Review your computer's status
Back up your computer
Find and fix problems

Control Panel ▸ System and Security ▸ Windows Update

Search Control Panel

Control Panel Home

Check for updates

Change settings —— **5**

View update history

Restore hidden updates

Updates: frequently asked questions

Windows Update

Install updates for your computer

1 important update is available

34 optional updates are available

1 important update selected, 5.1 MB

Install updates

Most recent check for updates: Today at 10:00 AM

Updates were installed: 6/1/2009 at 9:39 AM. View update history

You receive updates: For Windows and other products from Microsoft Update

Find out more about free software from Microsoft Update. Click here for details.

See also

Installed Updates

6 Configure the settings as shown here and click OK.

Control Panel ▶ System and Security ▶ Windows Update ▶ Change settings

Search Control Panel

Choose how Windows can install updates

When your computer is online, Windows can automatically check for important updates and install them using these settings. When new updates are available, you can also install them before shutting down the computer.

How does automatic updating help me?

6

Important updates

Install updates automatically (recommended)

Install new updates: Every day at 3:00 AM

Recommended updates

☑ Give me recommended updates the same way I receive important updates

Who can install updates

☑ Allow all users to install updates on this computer

Microsoft Update

☑ Give me updates for Microsoft products and check for new optional Microsoft software when I update Windows

Software notifications

☐ Show me detailed notifications when new Microsoft software is available

Note: Windows Update might update itself automatically first when checking for other updates. Read our privacy statement online.

OK   Cancel

? DID YOU KNOW?

If the computer is not online at 3 a.m., it will check for updates the next time it is.

! ALERT: You may see that optional components or updates are available. You can view these updates and install them if desired.

WHAT DOES THIS MEAN?

Windows Update: If enabled and configured properly, when you are online Windows 7 will check for security updates automatically and install them. You don't have to do anything and your PC is always updated with the latest security patches and features.

Scan for viruses with Windows Defender

You don't have to do much to Windows Defender except understand that it offers protection against Internet threats like malware. It's enabled by default and it runs in the background. However, if you ever think your computer has been attacked by an Internet threat (virus, worm, malware, etc.) you can run a manual scan here.

1 Open Windows Defender. (Click Start, type Defender and under Control Panel click Windows Defender.)

2 Click the arrow next to Scan (not the Scan icon). Click Full scan if you think the computer has been infected.

3 Click the X in the top right corner to close the Windows Defender window.

WHAT DOES THIS MEAN?
Malware: Stands for malicious software. Malware includes viruses, worms, spyware, etc.

Enable the firewall

Windows Firewall is a software program that checks the data that comes in from the Internet (or a local network) and then decides whether it's good data or bad. If it deems the data harmless, it will allow it to come though the firewall, if not, it's blocked.

1 Open Windows Firewall.

2 From the left pane, click Turn Windows Firewall on or off.

3 Verify the firewall is on. If not, select Turn on Windows Firewall. Review other settings.

4 Click OK.

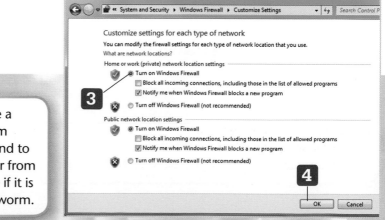

> **ALERT:** You have to have a firewall to keep hackers from getting access to your PC and to help prevent your computer from sending out malicious code if it is ever attacked by a virus or worm.

View and resolve Action Center warnings

Windows 7 tries hard to take care of your PC and your data. You'll see a pop-up if your anti-virus software is out of date (or not installed), if you don't have the proper security settings configured or if Windows Update or the firewall is disabled. You may get a user account control prompt each time you want to install a program or make a system-wide change.

1 Open the Action Center.

ALERT: When you see alerts, pay attention! You'll want to resolve them.

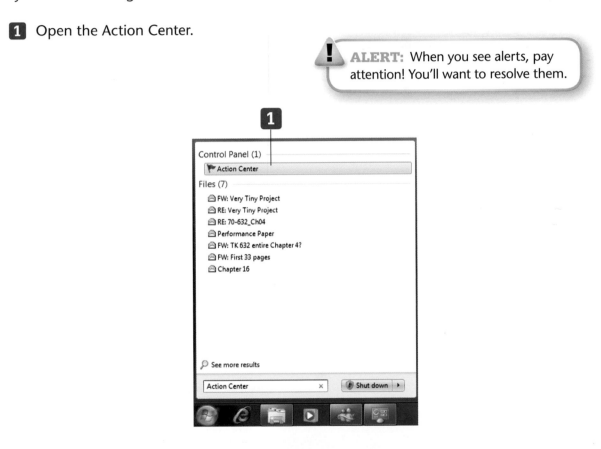

DID YOU KNOW?
Windows 7 comes with malware protection but not anti-virus protection.

ALERT: Install anti-virus software to protect your PC from viruses and worms.

2 If there's anything in red or yellow, click the down arrow (if necessary) to see the problem.

3 Click the button that offers the resolution suggestion to view the resolution option. Here these are Find a program online and More information.

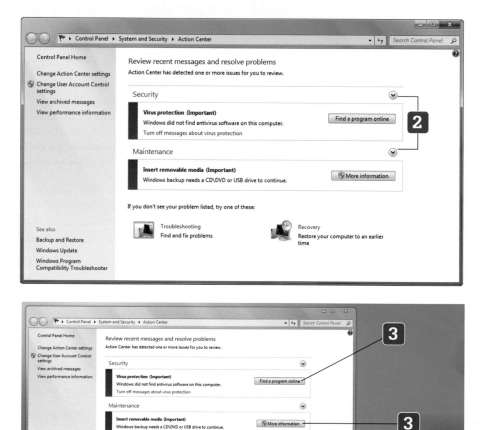

WHAT DOES THIS MEAN?

Virus: A self-replicating program that infects computers with intent to do harm. Viruses often come in the form of an attachment in an email.

Worm: A self-replicating program that infects computers with intent to do harm. However, unlike a virus, it does not need to attach itself to a running program.

Create a basic backup

Windows 7 comes with a backup program you can use to back up your personal data. The backup program is located in the Backup and Restore Center.

1 Open the Backup and Restore Center. (Click Start, type Backup.)

2 Click Set up backup. (Once it's set up, the button will change to Back up now.)

3 Choose a place to save your backup. Click Next.

Back up or restore user and system files

Backup

Windows Backup has not been set up.   [Set up backup...]

2

Restore

Windows could not find a backup for this computer.

Select another backup to restore files from

You can use the Recovery Control Panel to restore your computer to an earlier date.

Configure Backup

Select where you want to save your backup

We recommend that you save your backup on an external hard drive. Guidelines for choosing a backup destination

Backup locations:

Drive	Free Space	Total Size	
DVD RW Drive (D:)			

3

[Refresh]   [Add network location...]

ⓘ System images cannot be saved on this device. (More information)
The backed up data cannot be securely protected for this device. (More information)

[Next] [Cancel]

4 Select Let Windows choose (recommended).

5 Wait while the backup completes.

What do you want to back up?

4 ⦿ Let Windows choose (recommended)

Windows will back up data files saved in libraries, on the desktop, and in default Windows folders. These items will be backed up on a regular schedule. <u>How does Windows choose what files to back up?</u>

○ Let me choose

You can select libraries and folders and whether to include a system image in the backup. The items you choose will be backed up on a regular schedule.

[Next] [Cancel]

? DID YOU KNOW?
You can't create a backup on the hard disk of the computer you are backing up.

🔥 HOT TIP: Since backups can be large, consider a USB drive, external hard drive or DVD. You can also choose a network location.

? DID YOU KNOW?
You may be prompted to insert a blank DVD or a USB drive, depending on the choice made in Step 3.

8 Install hardware

Introduction

A new PC doesn't often come with everything you need. Most of the time it does not come with a preinstalled printer or scanner, and often you buy gadgets after the fact, like digital cameras or headphones. This hardware, as it's referred to, must be installed before it can be used. Additionally, the hardware's driver must be installed. A driver is a piece of software (or code) that allows the device to communicate with Windows 7 and vice versa. Drivers are different from software though and it's important to know the difference. In this chapter, you'll learn how to physically install printers, cameras and other hardware and how to make them work with Windows 7.

Install a digital camera or webcam

Most of the time, adding a camera is a simple affair. You insert the CD that came with the camera, plug in the new hardware and turn it on and wait for Windows 7 to install your hardware. However, it's always best to have directions for performing a task, so in that vein, I've included them here.

1. Read the directions that come with the camera. If there are specific instructions for installing the driver, follow them. If not, continue here.

2. Connect the camera to a wall outlet or insert fresh batteries and connect the camera to the PC using either a USB cable or a FireWire cable.

3. Insert the CD for the device if you have it; if a pop-up message appears, click the X to close the window.

4. Turn on the camera. Place it in Playback mode if that exists. Often, simply turning on the camera is enough.

5. Wait while the driver is installed.

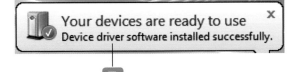

Your devices are ready to use   X
Device driver software installed successfully.

5

! ALERT: It's usually best to connect a new camera, turn it on and let Windows 7 install it. You need to intervene only when Windows 7 can't install the hardware on its own.

? DID YOU KNOW?
When you install everything on the CD that comes with your camera, you're probably installing applications you'll never use and don't need.

6 You'll see the camera in the Computer window (click Start, click Computer).

? DID YOU KNOW?
Even if you aren't installing the CD, leave the CD in the drive. If Windows 7 wants the information on the CD, it will acquire it.

WHAT DOES THIS MEAN?

Driver: Software that allows the PC and the new hardware to communicate with each other.

Software: A program that may not be required for the hardware to function correctly.

USB: A technology used to connect hardware to a PC. A USB cable is often used to connect a digital camera to a PC.

FireWire: A technology used to connect hardware to a PC. A FireWire cable is often used to connect a digital video camera to a PC.

Install a printer

Most of the time, adding a printer is as easy as installing a camera. You insert the CD that came with the printer, plug it in and turn it on and wait for Windows 7 to install it.

1 Connect the printer to a wall outlet.

2 Connect the printer to the PC using either a USB cable or a parallel port cable.

3 Insert the CD for the device if you have it.

4 If a pop-up message appears regarding the CD, click the X to close the window.

5 Turn on the device.

6 Wait while the driver is installed.

> **Your devices are ready to use** ✕
> Device driver software installed successfully.

6

! ALERT: It's usually best to connect the new printer, turn it on and let Windows 7 install it. You need to intervene only when 7 can't install the printer on its own.

? DID YOU KNOW?
When you install everything on the CD that comes with your printer, you're probably installing applications you'll never use and don't need.

! ALERT: Read the directions that come with each new device you acquire. If there are specific instructions for installing the driver on a Windows 7 PC, follow those directions, not the generic directions offered here.

? DID YOU KNOW?
Leave the CD in the drive. If Windows 7 wants the information on the CD, it will acquire it from there.

HOT TIP: You will need to install the printer software (see image below) if you want to access advanced printer preferences such as printing in reverse or applying light or heavy ink.

Hewlett-Packard Photosmart Printer Series

Welcome to the Install Wizard for Hewlett-Packard Photosmart Printer Series

The Install Wizard will install Hewlett-Packard Photosmart Printer Series on your computer. To continue, click Next.

WARNING: This program is protected by copyright law and international treaties.

Before clicking Next, please save all of your work, close any open programs, and temporarily disable your anti-virus program.

< Back | Next > | Cancel

DID YOU KNOW?
USB is a faster connection than a parallel port, but FireWire is faster than both.

ALERT: Always remain aware of what you're installing. Install drivers only and then install software if you find you need it.

Install other hardware

For hardware other than printers or cameras, perform the same steps. Insert a driver CD if one came with the hardware, plug in the new hardware and turn it on and wait for Windows 7 to install the required driver. If Windows 7 can't find the driver it needs on the CD or in its own driver database on the hard drive, it will connect to the Internet and look for the driver in Microsoft's online driver database. Almost all of the time, Windows 7 will be successful using one of these methods. For the most part, speakers, headphones, printers, scanners and digital cameras all install this way.

1 Connect the hardware to a PC and/or a wall outlet.

2 Insert the CD for the device if you have it.

3 If a pop-up message appears regarding the CD, click the X to close the window.

4 Turn on the device.

5 Wait while the driver is installed.

6 If you receive a message that the driver was not successfully installed, click the message to see why and how to resolve the issue.

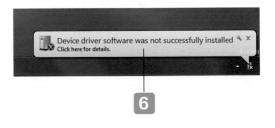

| Your devices are ready to use |
| Device driver software installed successfully. |

5

| Device driver software was not successfully installed |
| Click here for details. |

6

ALERT: On occasion, hardware manufacturers will require you to install software first and then plug in the device and turn on the hardware, so read the instructions that came with your hardware to know what order to do what, just as a precaution.

ALERT: When the instructions for a hardware device tell you to install the CD before connecting the hardware, it's often just a ruse to get you to install unnecessary software, so be aware of what you're installing.

Locate a driver

As noted, almost all of the time hardware installs automatically and with no input from you (other than plugging it in and turning it on). However, in rare cases, the hardware does not install properly or is simply not available. If this happens, you'll be informed that the hardware did not install and may not work properly. If you cannot replace the device with something Windows 7 recognises, you'll have to locate and install the driver yourself.

1 Write down the name and model number of the device.

2 Open Internet Explorer and locate the manufacturer's website.

3 Locate a link for Support, Support and Drivers, Customer Support or something similar. Click it.

4 Locate your device driver by make, model or other characteristics.

HOT TIP: To find the manufacturer's website, try putting a www. before the company name and a .com after. (www. epson.com, www.hewlett-packard.com and www.apple.com are examples.)

ALERT: Locating a driver is the first step. You must now download the driver and, later, install it.

HOT TIP: The make and model of a device are probably located on the bottom of the device.

Download and install a driver

If you've located the driver you need, you can now download and install it. Downloading is the process of saving the driver to your computer's hard drive. Once downloaded, you can install the driver.

1 Locate the driver as detailed in the previous section.

2 Click Download Driver, Obtain Software or something similar.

3 Click Save.

4 Click Run, Install or Open Window to begin the installation.

5 Follow the directions in the set-up process to complete the installation.

HOT TIP: Save the file in a location you recognise, like Downloads.

ALERT: If installation does not begin automatically, browse to the location of the file and double-click it to begin the installation manually.

Use ReadyBoost

ReadyBoost is a technology that lets you add more RAM (random access memory) to a PC easily, without opening the computer tower or the laptop case. Adding RAM often improves performance dramatically. ReadyBoost lets you use a USB flash drive or a secure digital memory card (like the one in your digital camera) as RAM if it meets certain requirements.

1 Insert a USB flash drive, thumb drive, portable music player or memory card into an available slot on the outside of your PC.

2 Wait while Windows 7 checks to see whether the device can perform as memory.

3 If prompted to use the flash drive or memory card to improve system performance, click Speed up my system.

ALERT: USB keys must be at least USB 2.0 and have at last 64 MB of free space, but don't worry about that, you'll be told if the hardware isn't up to par.

HOT TIP: Only newer and larger USB keys will work for ReadyBoost.

WHAT DOES THIS MEAN?

RAM: Random access memory is where information is stored temporarily so the operating system has quick access to it. The more RAM you have, the better your PC should perform.

USB or thumb drive: A small device that plugs into a USB port on your PC, often for the purpose of backing up or storing files on external media.

Portable music player: Often a small USB drive. This device also has a headphone jack and controls for listening to music stored on it.

Media card: A removable card used in digital cameras to store data and transfer it to the PC.

Install software

As with installing hardware, software installation goes smoothly almost every time. Just make sure you get your software from a reliable source, like Amazon, Microsoft's website, Apple's website (think iTunes, not software for Macs only) or a retail store. Downloading software from the Internet is risky and you never know if it will run properly or contain adware or spyware. It's best to simply stay away, unless the company is well known like Adobe and you're willing to burn your own software backup disks.

1 Insert the CD or DVD in the appropriate drive; if prompted, click Run or Install.

2 If you are not prompted:
- Click Start.
- Click Computer.
- Right-click the CD or DVD drive.
- Click Install or run program from your media.

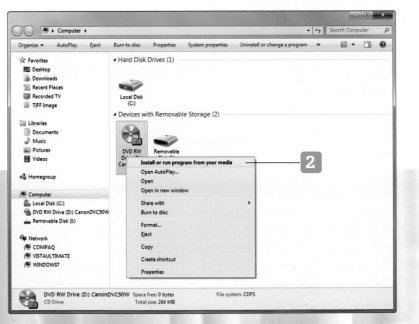

3 Work through the installation wizard.

Canon Digital Video Solution Disk   **X**

Choose Destination Location
Select folder where Setup will install files.

Setup will install Solution Disk in the following folder.

To install to this folder, click Next. To install to a different folder, click Browse and select another folder.

3

┌─ Destination Folder ───────────────────────────────────┐

  C:\Program Files\Canon\   Browse...

InstallShield ───

                        < Back   Next >   Cancel

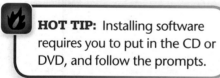

HOT TIP: Installing software requires you to put in the CD or DVD, and follow the prompts.

ALERT: If you aren't prompted to install the software, click Start and Computer, then manually start the installation.

9 Windows Media Player

Introduction

Windows Media Player offers all you'll need to manage your music library, get music online and copy the CDs from your own music collection to your PC. You can also use it to burn music CDs you can listen to in your car, share music using your local network and more.

Open Media Player and locate music

You open Media Player the same way you open other programs, from the Start menu. Once opened, you'll need to know where the Library button is so that you can access different kinds of media. We'll start with music.

1. Open Media Player from the taskbar.

2. Click the arrow next to the Library button.

3. Click Music. (This is really a moot point because Music is the default, but you need to know how to get here to switch to other media libraries.)

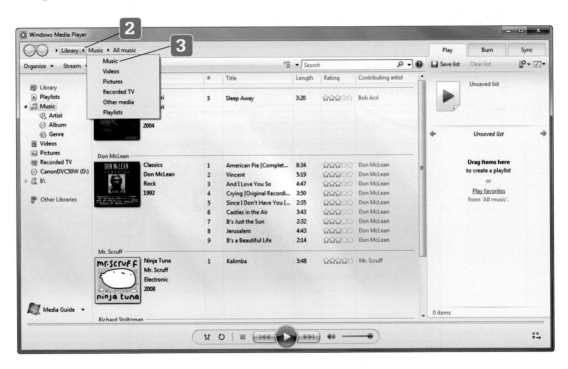

? DID YOU KNOW?

You can select Videos, Pictures, Recorded TV, Other media and Playlists too.

WHAT DOES THIS MEAN?

Windows Media Player: An application included with Windows 7. You can watch DVDs and videos here, listen to and manage music and even listen to radio stations or view pictures.

Listen to a song

To play any music track, simply navigate to it and double-click it. Songs are listed in the Navigation pane.

1 Open Media Player, if necessary, click the Library button and choose Music.

2 Click Album. (Note you can also click Artist, Genre or any other category to locate a song.)

3 Double-click any album to play it.

4 Double-click any song on the album to play it.

Double-click a song to play it.

This line shows the song's progress.

Edit a song title and other information

Occasionally, the song title or album title won't be correct. You can edit any data related to a song or album by right-clicking it.

 In Media Player, locate the song or album title to change.

2 Right-click the song and click Edit.

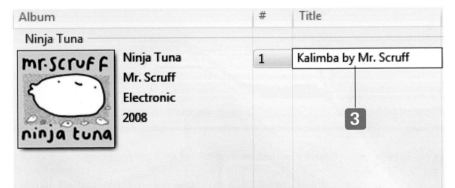

3 Type a new title for the song or album.

4 Press Enter on the keyboard.

Copy a CD to your hard drive

You can copy CDs to your hard drive. This is called 'ripping'. To rip means to copy in media-speak. Once music is on your PC, you can listen to it in Media Player, burn compilations of music to other CDs and even put the music on a portable music player.

1 Insert the CD to copy into the CD drive.

2 Deselect any songs you do not want to copy to your PC.

3 In Windows Media Player, click the Rip CD button.

HOT TIP: You can watch the rip progress in the List pane.

DID YOU KNOW?
You have the right to rip any CD you own to your PC for no extra cost.

DID YOU KNOW?
By default, music is saved in your Music folder.

Copy files to a CD

There are two ways to take music with you when you are on the road or on the go. You can copy the music to a portable device like a music player or you can create your own CDs, choosing the songs to copy and placing them on the CD in the desired order.

1 Open Media Player.

2 Insert a blank CD and click the Burn tab.

3 Click any song title or album to add and drag it to the List pane.

4 When you've added the songs you want, click Start Burn.

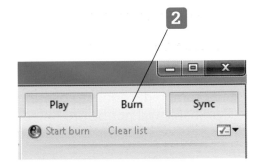

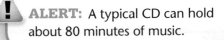

? DID YOU KNOW?
Look at the slider in the List pane to see how much room is left on the CD.

! ALERT: A typical CD can hold about 80 minutes of music.

WHAT DOES THIS MEAN?
Burn: A term used to describe the process of copying music from a computer to a CD.

Watch a DVD

You can watch a DVD on your computer just as you would on any DVD player. Windows 7 offers two choices for doing so, Windows Media Center and Windows Media Player. We'll talk about Windows Media Player here.

1 Find the button on the PC's tower, keyboard or laptop that opens the DVD drive door. Press it.

2 Place the DVD in the door and press the button again to close it.

3 If prompted, choose to play the DVD movie using Windows Media Player. You probably will not be prompted.

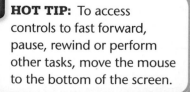 **HOT TIP:** To access controls to fast forward, pause, rewind or perform other tasks, move the mouse to the bottom of the screen.

HOT TIP: The controls you'll see and use in Media Player are very similar to (and perhaps exactly like) the controls you see on your own DVD player.

Create a playlist

Playlists allow you to organise songs the way you like to listen to them. You might consider creating playlists that contain songs specific to an occasion, like a dinner party, after-pub party, wedding shower or similar. Then, when the event happens, you can simply put on the playlist and let the music take care of itself.

1 Open Windows Media Player and click Create playlist.

 HOT TIP: You'll have to navigate to Artist, Album or Genre to locate the songs to add, so when dragging, drag to the new playlist in the Navigation pane.

2 When you click Create playlist, the type will turn blue. Type the name of the playlist here. My playlist is named Party Music. The new playlist name will appear under Playlists.

3 Locate any song or album to add to the playlist.

4 Drag (and drop) these to the new playlist.

5 Continue to drag and drop songs as desired.

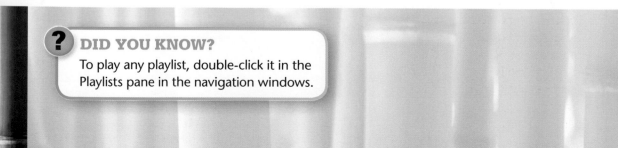

? DID YOU KNOW?

To play any playlist, double-click it in the Playlists pane in the navigation windows.

Share your music library

If you have more than one PC in your home and those PCs are networked, you can share your media library with them. Sharing allows you to keep only one copy of media (music, videos, pictures) on one PC, while sharing it with other PCs running Windows Media Player, various media extenders and Microsoft's Xbox 360.

1 Open Windows Media Player and click the Stream button.

2 Choose the streaming options you desire.

3 To see additional options, click the Stream button again and choose More streaming options.

4 Configure options as desired and click OK when finished.

ALERT: The Windows 7 PC that stores the media you want to share must be connected to your home network. The network must be private.

HOT TIP: In the Media streaming options window, note that you can choose homegroup and sharing options, choose power options and learn more about media streaming, among other things.

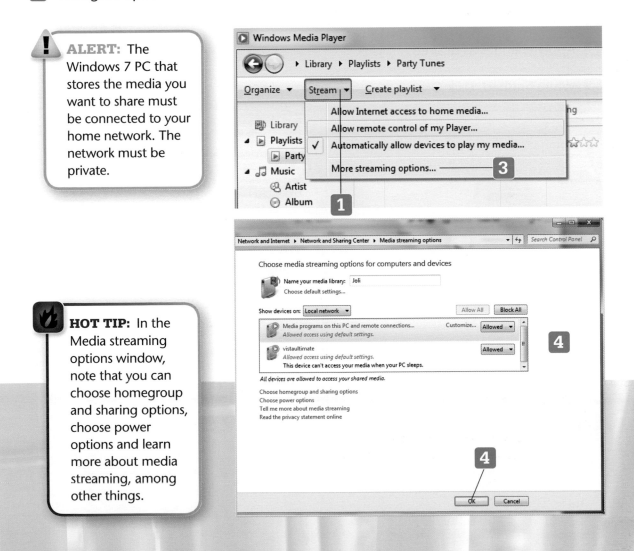

Configure options

You may want to tweak the options available in Media Player. There are lots of options to consider, especially the ones related to privacy.

1 Open Media Player.

2 Click Tools, then Options. (If you can't see the Tools menu, click the Alt key on the keyboard.)

3 From the Options dialogue box, click the tabs to view the options.

4 Apply changes as desired.

5 When finished, click OK.

HOT TIP: Click the Help button at the bottom of any tab to learn more.

10 Windows Live Photo Gallery

Introduction

Windows Live Photo Gallery may be all you need to manage, manipulate, view and share your digital photos. Before you install additional software, including software that was included on the CD that shipped with your digital camera, printer or scanner, try this program. It's free and only requires you to download and install it.

Download and install Windows Live Photo Gallery

If you've never downloaded and/or installed a program before, you may be a little nervous about doing so. Don't worry, it's really easy, and Microsoft has set it up so that the process requires very little input from you. There are only a few steps: go to the website, click the Download link and wait for the download and installation process to complete.

1 Open Internet Explorer and go to http://www.windowslive.com/ Desktop/PhotoGallery.

2 Look for the Download now button and click it. You'll be prompted to click Download now once more on the next screen.

3 Click Run and when prompted, click Yes.

4 When prompted, select the items to download. You can select all of the items some of the items, or only Windows Photo Gallery. Click Install. You may find you have already installed Windows Photo Gallery, as shown here, if you installed the Live suite in Chapter 6.

5 When prompted to select your settings, make the desired choices. You can't go wrong here – there are no bad options.

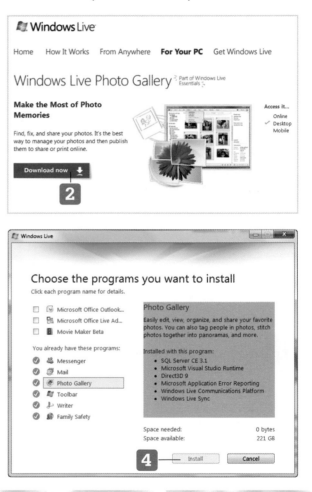

HOT TIP: Select Mail, Photo Gallery and Toolbar for best results. We'll be covering these programs in this book.

? DID YOU KNOW?
It's OK to select all of these programs if you think you'll use them; they are all free.

HOT TIP: If you installed Windows Live Mail in Chapter 6, you may have already installed Windows Live Photo Gallery.

Get a Windows Live account

When you use 'Live' services, like Windows Live Mail, Windows Live Photo Gallery and others, you have to log in to them using a Windows Live account. This account is free and you can use it to sign in to Live-related websites on the Internet. You need a Windows Live account. A Windows Live account is an email address and password you use to log on to your Live programs on the Internet.

1 If you do not already have a Windows Live account, click Sign up after the installation of Live Mail completes. (You can also go to https://signup.live.com.)

2 Fill out the required information and click I accept when finished.

> **Windows** Live
>
> ### Welcome to Windows Live!
>
> **Your new programs are in the Windows Live folder on the Start menu.**
>
> #### Do you have a Windows Live ID?
> To get the most from your new programs, use your Windows Live ID to sign in.
> If you use Hotmail, Messenger, or Xbox LIVE, you already have a Windows Live ID. If not, it only takes a minute to sign up.
>
> Sign up ——————————— **1**
>
> Close

HOT TIP: Fill out the information with true information. This is an ID, after all.

? DID YOU KNOW?
You can use your Windows Live email account as a regular email address, or simply use it to log into Live services on the Internet.

> ### Create your Windows Live ID
> It gets you into all Windows Live services—and other places you see
> All information is required.
>
> **1** Already using **Hotmail**, **Messenger**, or **Xbox LIVE**? Sign in now
>
> Use your e-mail address: *Example: someone@example.com*
> Or get a Windows Live e-mail address
> Create a password:
> 6-character minimum; case sensitive
> Retype password:
> First name:
> Last name:
> Country/region: United States
> State: Select one
> ZIP code:
> Gender: ○ Male ○ Female
> Birth year: *Example: 1990*
>
> *B9VP9NE6*
>
> Characters:
> Enter the 8 characters you see

2

View pictures

You can use various applications to view pictures with Windows 7, but Windows Live Photo Gallery is the best. With it, you have easy access to slide shows, editing tools and picture groupings. You can sort and filter and organise as desired.

1 Open Windows Live Photo Gallery. If prompted, log in using your Windows Live ID.

2 If prompted, click Yes to associate picture file types with Windows Live Photo Gallery.

3 Notice the sample pictures. Double-click any picture to open it in a larger window.

4 Click Back to Gallery to return to the previous page.

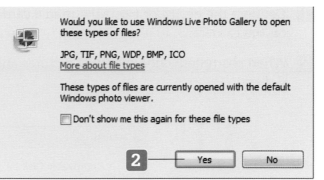

> Would you like to use Windows Live Photo Gallery to open these types of files?
>
> JPG, TIF, PNG, WDP, BMP, ICO
> More about file types
>
> These types of files are currently opened with the default Windows photo viewer.
>
> ☐ Don't show me this again for these file types
>
> **2** ──── Yes   No

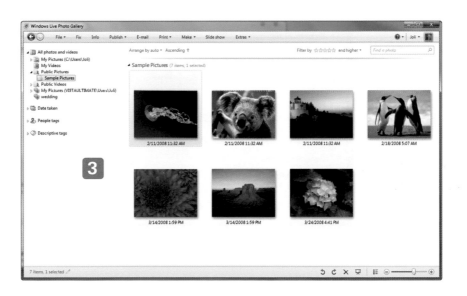

DID YOU KNOW?

Your digital pictures are stored in the Pictures folder on your hard drive, not 'in' or 'by' Photo Gallery. Photo Gallery offers a place to view and work with images – it has nothing to do with how they are stored on the PC.

DID YOU KNOW?

You can click Start, All Programs, then Windows Live Photo Gallery or you can type Photo in the Start Search window.

Import pictures from a digital camera or media card

After you've taken pictures with your digital camera, you'll want to move or copy those pictures to the PC. Once stored on the PC's hard drive, you can view, edit, email or print the pictures (among other things).

1 Connect the device or insert the media card into the card reader. If applicable, turn on the camera.

2 When prompted, choose Import pictures and videos using Windows Live Photo Gallery.

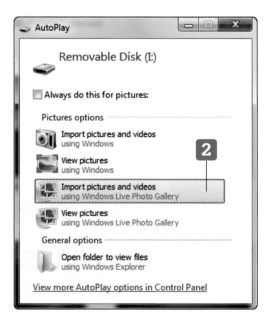

SEE ALSO: Install a digital camera or webcam, Chapter 8.

? DID YOU KNOW?

These steps work for importing pictures from a mobile phone too.

3 Click Import all new items now.

4 Type a descriptive name for the group of pictures you're importing and click Import.

5 View your new photos.

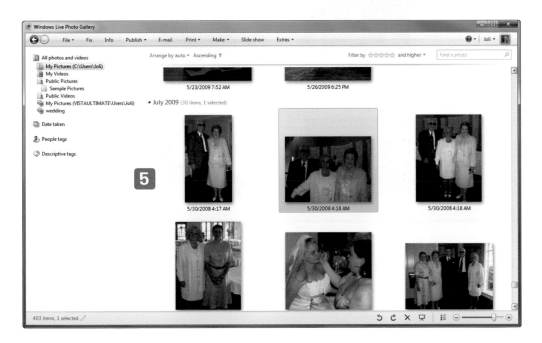

HOT TIP: If desired, tick Erase after importing. This will cause Windows 7 to erase the images from the device after the import is complete.

ALERT: If your device isn't recognised when you plug it in and turn it on, in Windows Live Photo Gallery click File, then click Import from a camera or scanner.

Play a slideshow of pictures

1 Open Windows Live Photo Gallery.

2 Select any folder that contains pictures.

3 Click the Slide Show button. Wait at least three seconds.

4 To end the show, press the Esc key on the keyboard.

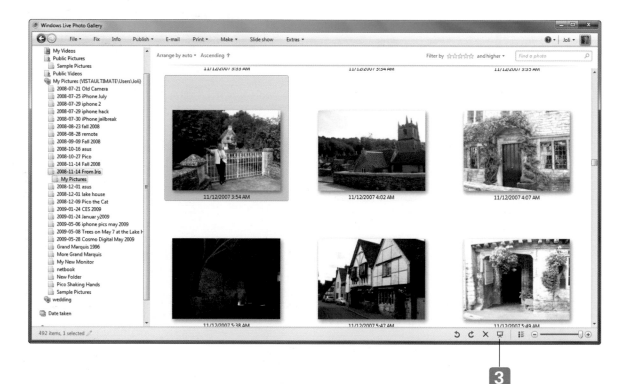

3

HOT TIP: Press the F11 key on the keyboard to start a slide show.

HOT TIP: If you haven't added any of your own photos yet, use the sample pictures to view a slide show.

Auto adjust picture quality

With pictures now on your PC and available in Windows Live Photo Gallery, you can perform some editing. Photo Gallery offers the ability to correct brightness and contrast, colour temperature, tint and saturation, among other things.

1 Open Photo Gallery.

2 Double-click a picture to edit.

3 Click Fix.

4 Click Auto adjust to fix problems with the photo. Adjustments will be made automatically.

5 Continue adjusting as desired, using the sliders to adjust the settings.

HOT TIP: Click the Back to gallery button and your changes will be saved automatically.

HOT TIP: When you select a 'fix' option, options will appear on the right side. You can apply the options as desired.

ALERT: After applying any option, to see more options click the down and up arrows that will appear in the right pane.

Crop a picture

To crop means to remove parts of a picture you don't want by allowing you to reposition the picture and remove extraneous parts. You can also rotate the frame.

1 Open Photo Gallery.

2 Select a picture to crop.

3 Click Fix.

4 Click Crop photo.

5 Drag the corners of the box to resize it and drag the entire box to move it around in the picture.

6 Click Apply.

HOT TIP: Click the arrow next to Custom to apply a preconfigured size.

HOT TIP: Click Rotate frame to change the position of the crop box.

Add information to a picture

You can add information about a picture by adding 'tags'. Tags you create are words that describe the picture. Once tags are added, you can filter, sort and organise your pictures using these tags.

1 Open Windows Live Photo Gallery.

2 Right-click any picture and click Properties.

3 Click Tags.

4 Type a tag name or several tag names separated by semicolons.

5 Click OK.

HOT TIP: Pictures can have multiple tags. You might tag a photo as Holiday, but also apply tags that name the people in the picture, the city or the country.

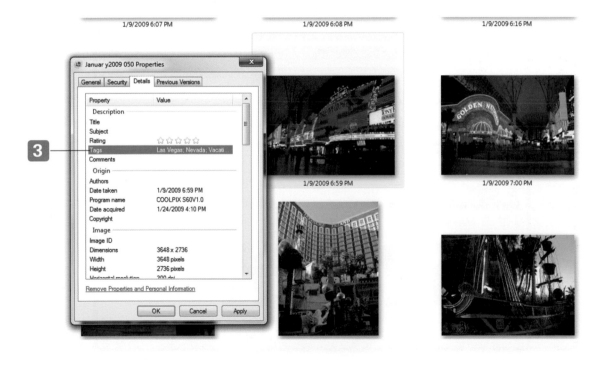

? DID YOU KNOW?
Some tags are applied automatically when you import pictures from a digital camera, including the date they were uploaded, along with any name you applied to the imported group.

HOT TIP: You'll see the new tags under Descriptive tags in the Windows Live Photo Gallery interface on the bottom left.

Email a picture

You can email photos you want to share from inside Photo Gallery. You can also choose the size to email them, apply effects to the photos, autocorrect the photos and more.

1 Open Windows Live Photo Gallery.

2 Select pictures to email.

3 Click E-mail.

4 Use the options available to apply effects, change the resolution of the photo, use autocorrect and more.

5 Compose the email and send it.

HOT TIP: Click any arrows to see more options. You can see a double arrow here next to Spotlight. Click it to view more options.

SEE ALSO: Compose and send an email, Chapter 6.

Print a picture

You can share a picture by printing it. Again, you can print from inside Photo Gallery.

1 Open Photo Gallery.

2 Select a picture to print. (You can also double-click the image as I've done here.)

3 Click Print.

4 Click Print again.

5 Using the Print Pictures wizard, select the type and number of prints to create.

6 Click Print.

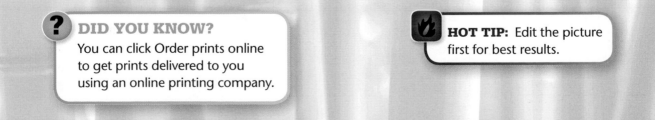

DID YOU KNOW? You can click Order prints online to get prints delivered to you using an online printing company.

HOT TIP: Edit the picture first for best results.

Add folders to Windows Live Photo Gallery

Photo Gallery looks for digital files in four places: My Pictures, Public Pictures, My Videos and Public Videos. If you've created your own folders outside of these four places and put pictures in them, you'll have to tell Photo Gallery where those folders are.

1 Open Windows Live Photo Gallery.

2 Click File and click Include a folder in the gallery.

3 Expand the 'trees' to locate the folder to add.

4 Click OK.

5 Click OK in the dialogue box that appears.

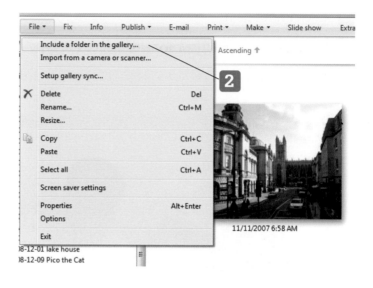

Personalise Windows Live Photo Gallery

You can personalise Windows Live Photo Gallery quickly and easily. You can change the size of the picture thumbnails, what information is shown with the thumbnails and more.

1 In Windows Live Photo Gallery, use the slider to change the size of the thumbnails.

2 Right-click an empty area of the interface, click View and choose what else should be shown with the thumbnails.

3 Click Extras and click Download more photo tools to get additional editing features.

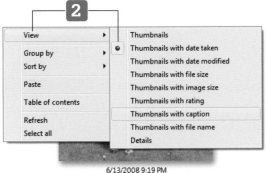

6/13/2008 9:19 PM

6/13/2008 9:19 PM

11 Windows Media Center

Introduction

Windows Media Center is installed on the three most popular Windows 7 editions: Home Premium, Professional and Ultimate. Media Center is a one-stop media application that lets you access and manage pictures, videos, movies, music, online media, television, DVDs and CDs and radio.

Media Center really stands out for watching cable and Internet TV and online media, and watching DVDs you own or rent. It's a place to enjoy the media you already have access to and have already 'managed' in other applications (like Windows Live Photo Gallery or Media Player). Media Center has an online TV guide to help you find out what's available to watch and when, and you can record television programmes, pause live TV and then fast-forward or rewind through what you've paused and recorded.

You should start with Media Center by watching and recording TV, then move on to watching DVDs and viewing online media. As time passes and you get more comfortable with Media Center, you may find you prefer it to Media Player and Photo Gallery for managing other media too.

Open Media Center

Before you open Media Center for the first time, make sure you have a working Internet connection, speakers, a CD/DVD drive and a TV tuner installed and in working order for best performance.

1 Click Start.

2 Click Windows Media Center. You'll also find Media Center from Start and All Programs.

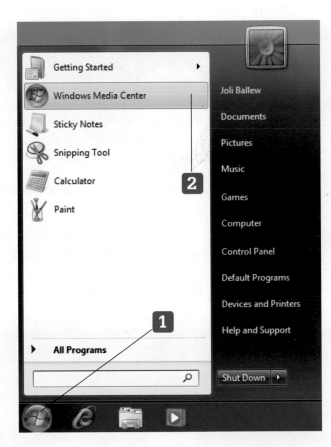

 ALERT: Not all computers come with a TV tuner. If your computer does not, you won't be able to watch live TV.

HOT TIP: Media Center's interface includes several menus: TV, Movies, Sports, Tasks, Extras, Pictures + Videos and Music.

Set up Media Center

The first time you open Media Center, you'll be prompted to set it up. The easiest set-up is to choose Express.

1 Open Media Center.

2 When you see the Set Up screen shown here, click Continue.

3 When prompted, click Express.

Set up a TV signal

To watch live TV, you have to tell Media Center how you connect to your TV signal (and your PC has to have a TV tuner). There are many ways to watch TV, including but not limited to using an antenna, using a cable box, making a connection directly from a coaxial connection in the wall, using a satellite dish and more.

1 Use the arrow keys on the keyboard or remote control to locate TV and live TV setup.

2 Choose the options that apply to your TV set-up and connection. You may have to input a postcode, choose what type of connection you use or answer other questions regarding your television service.

3 As prompted, make the proper choices, working through the wizard. Click Finish when done.

HOT TIP: Once the signal is set up, Windows Media Center will download information for up to 14 days of TV programming. You can use the results to record and watch television.

ALERT: Because each option results in a personalised 'next step' when setting up your TV signal, there's no way to work through each scenario here.

Watch, pause and rewind live TV

When you open Media Center, TV is the default option and Recorded TV is selected. To watch live television, you'll need to use the mouse, keyboard or remote control to move one place to the right to live TV. While watching live TV, you can watch, pause and rewind the show you're watching (and fast-forward through previously paused programming).

1 Open Media Center.

2 Move once to the right of recorded TV and click live tv.

3 Position the mouse at the bottom of the live TV screen to show the controls.

4 Use the controls to manage live TV.

Channel down | Channel up | Play/pause | Mute | Volume down

Record | Stop | Rewind | Fast-forward | Volume up

HOT TIP: Press pause at the beginning of a 30-minute show for 10 minutes and you can fast-forward through the commercials. (For a 60-minute show, pause for 20 minutes.)

ALERT: Stop watching TV by clicking the Stop button.

Obtain programme information

When you're watching live TV, you'll see the broadcast, of course, but other items will appear and disappear, based on where you move the mouse. The show's broadcast information appears when you change to the channel and you can also bring it up by right-clicking an area of the screen.

1 Open Media Center.

2 Under TV, click live tv.

3 Right-click anywhere on the screen to access additional information about the show.

 HOT TIP: Miss something? Drag the slider to the left to rewind live TV.

HOT TIP: Click the right or left arrows for more information about the show, to turn on closed captioning, to see a synopsis of the show and more.

Record a future TV show

You can click the Record button while watching live TV to record the show you're watching. You won't always want to record what you're watching though; you will more likely want to record something that is coming on later in the week. That's what the Guide is for.

1 Open Media Center.

2 Under TV, move right and click guide.

3 Locate a show to record.

4 Right-click the programme.

5 Select Record.

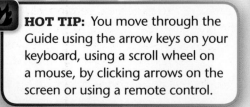

HOT TIP: You move through the Guide using the arrow keys on your keyboard, using a scroll wheel on a mouse, by clicking arrows on the screen or using a remote control.

HOT TIP: Use the Back button to navigate through Media Center.

Record a future TV series

When you record a series, you record every show related to the series. You can tell Media Center to record all shows (including reruns) or just new ones, among other options.

1 Open Media Center.

2 Under TV, move right and click guide.

3 Locate a show to record.

4 Right-click the programme.

5 Click Record Series. It's just below Record.

HOT TIP: You move through the Guide using the arrow keys on your keyboard, using a scroll wheel on a mouse, by clicking arrows on the screen or using a remote control.

ALERT: If another show is set to record during this time, you'll be alerted to a 'conflict' and will have to configure which of the conflicting programmes should record.

HOT TIP: To cancel a recording, click the programme and click Do Not Record. To stop recording a series, click Series Info and Cancel Series.

Watch a recorded TV show

To watch a television show you've recorded, simply browse to TV, Recorded TV and click the recorded show you want to watch.

1 Open Media Center and under TV, click recorded TV.

2 Locate the programme to watch.

3 Click the show you want and click Watch.

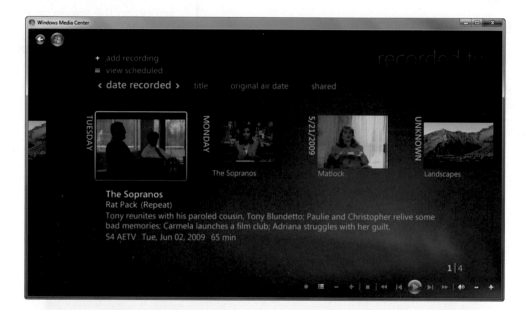

 **ALERT:** Right-click and select Settings to view additional options.

? DID YOU KNOW?
When you record a series, a folder will be created for it that will hold the related shows.

🔥 HOT TIP: You can pause, rewind and fast-forward a recorded TV show in the same manner as watching live TV.

View your pictures

Although you can use Windows Live Photo Gallery to view your pictures, you may find you like Media Center better.

1 Open Media Center.

2 Scroll to Pictures + Videos and click picture library.

3 Browse through the available pictures and picture folders.

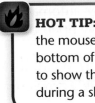

HOT TIP: Position the mouse at the bottom of the screen to show the controls during a slide show.

4 Click play slide show to play a slide show of the pictures in that folder.

Watch a DVD

You know you can watch a DVD in Media Player and you can also watch a DVD in Media Center. By default, a DVD will play in Media Player though, so if it opens in Media Player automatically when you insert the DVD, you'll have to close that window and manually open the DVD in Media Center.

1 Make sure Windows Media Center is open and put a DVD in the DVD drive.

2 If the DVD does not play automatically, under Movies, select play dvd.

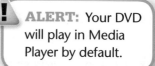

ALERT: Your DVD will play in Media Player by default.

3 Use the mouse, remote control or arrow on the keyboard to play the movie, view special features or select other options.

4 Use the controls introduced earlier to pause, stop, rewind and fast-forward through the movie.

Listen to music

You know you can listen to music in Media Player and you can also listen to music in Media Center.

1 Open Media Center.

2 Scroll to Music and click music library.

3 Locate the album to play. (You can also put a music CD in the CD drive.)

4 Click Play Album or select any other option.

5 While the music is playing, click Visualize.

? DID YOU KNOW?
You can click artists, genres, songs, playlists and more to refine the list.

? DID YOU KNOW?
Click Shuffle to play the songs on the album or playlist in random order.

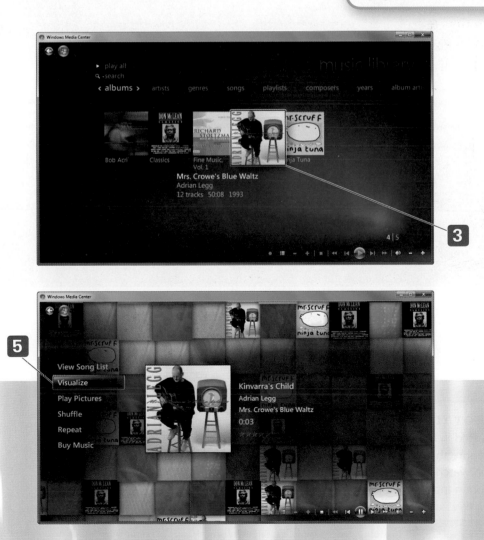

Explore Internet TV

Under Extras, you'll find Internet tv. You can watch quite a few shows on Internet TV, provided you have a working internet connection.

1 Open Media Center.

2 Click Extras and select internet tv.

3 Browse the offerings and when you find something you like, click it to watch.

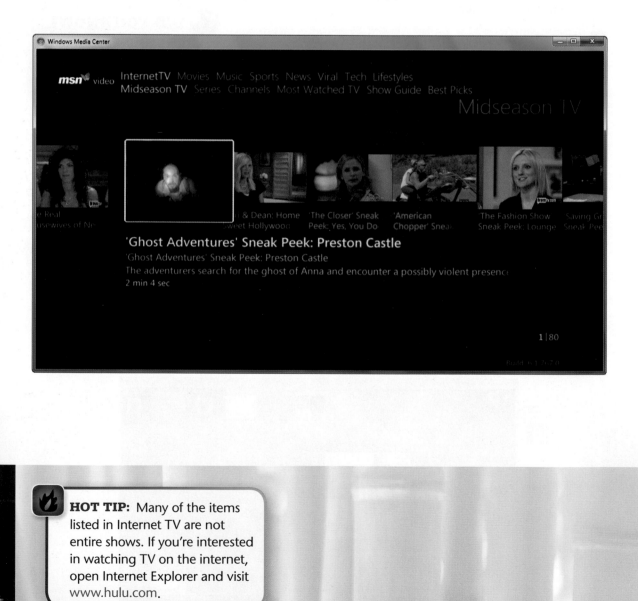

HOT TIP: Many of the items listed in Internet TV are not entire shows. If you're interested in watching TV on the internet, open Internet Explorer and visit www.hulu.com.

12 Change system defaults

Introduction

Windows 7 comes preconfigured with certain settings called system defaults. These include things like the mouse pointer type and speed, how much idle time should pass before the computer goes to sleep and how folders look on the screen. You can make changes to these defaults along with other settings automatically configured, such as the date and time, the language, what happens when you insert a DVD into the DVD drive and similar.

Change AutoPlay settings

Windows 7 makes a decision each time you insert a blank CD a DVD movie, a picture CD or a music CD by opening the program it thinks you will most probably want to use. Alternatively, you may be prompted each time regarding your preference. You can tell Windows 7 what you want it to do when you insert or access media though, and configure what program should be used to open what type of media (and to open it in that program automatically).

1 Click Start.

2 Click Default Programs. (It's on the Start menu.)

3 Click Change AutoPlay settings.

4 Use the drop-down lists to select the program to use for the media you want to play.

5 Click Save.

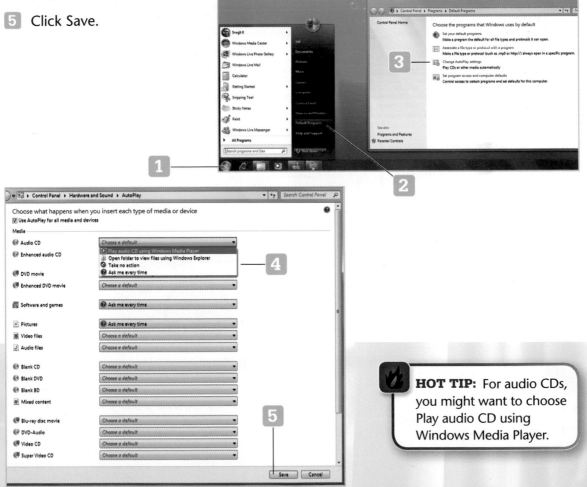

HOT TIP: For audio CDs, you might want to choose Play audio CD using Windows Media Player.

Change the date and time

If there is ever a need to change the date and time (or the time zone), you can do so from the Date and Time dialogue box.

1 Click Start.

2 Click Control Panel.

3 Click Clock, Language, and Region.

4 Click Set the time and date.

5 Click Change date and time.

6 Use the arrows or type in a new time.

7 Select a new date.

8 Click OK.

9 Click OK.

HOT TIP: Click the Additional Clocks tab to add a second clock in a different time zone.

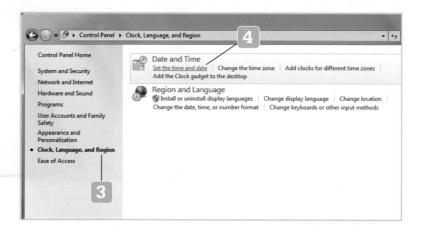

HOT TIP: Choose Change the time zone to change the time zone instead of the time.

Change language settings

When you travel with a laptop computer, you may need to change the country or region, the date, time and number format. If you speak and work in multiple languages, you may also need to change keyboards or other input methods. You can do this from the Control Panel.

1 Click Start.

2 Click Control Panel.

3 Click Region and Language.

4 Work through each tab, starting with the Formats tab.

5 Make changes as desired from the available drop-down lists.

6 Click OK.

4

Region and Language

| Formats | Location | Keyboards and Languages | Administrative |

Format:

English (United States)

Date and time formats

5

Short date:	M/d/yyyy
Long date:	dddd, MMMM dd, yyyy
Short time:	h:mm tt
Long time:	h:mm:ss tt
First day of week:	Sunday

What does the notation mean?

Examples

Short date:	6/3/2009
Long date:	Wednesday, June 03, 2009
Short time:	1:33 PM
Long time:	1:33:31 PM

Additional settings...

Go online to learn about changing languages and regional formats

OK   Cancel   Apply

Region and Language

| Formats | Location | Keyboards and Languages | Administrative |

Some software, including Windows, may provide you with additional content for a particular location. Some services provide local information such as news and weather.

Current location:

United Kingdom

6

See also

Default location

OK   Cancel   Apply

? DID YOU KNOW?
You can customise any format by clicking the Customize this format button.

🔥 HOT TIP: To set your current location, click the Current location tab and select the desired country from the drop-down list.

Change folder options

You can change how folders look using Folder Options. You can use a single-click (instead of a double-click) to open a folder, choose to open each folder in its own window, view hidden files and folders and more.

1 Click Start.

2 In the Start Search window, type Folder Options.

3 Under Programs in the results list, click Folder Options.

4 From the General tab, read the options and make changes as desired.

5 From the View tab, read the options and make changes as desired.

6 From the Search tab, read the options and make changes as desired.

HOT TIP: To shorten the list of search results, deselect Find partial matches.

HOT TIP: Select Always show menus and every folder will offer menus where available.

Change mouse settings

The speed the mouse moves, the pointer shape, vertical scrolling and other mouse options are all configured with default settings. You can change the settings, perhaps turning a right-handed mouse into a left-handed mouse using Mouse settings.

1 Click Start and in the Start Search window, type mouse.

2 In the results, under Programs, click Mouse.

3 From the Buttons tab, read the options and make changes as desired.

4 From the Pointers tab, select a theme as desired.

5 From the Pointer Options tab, read the options and make changes as desired.

6 From the Wheel tab, read the options and make changes as desired.

7 Click OK.

HOT TIP: Enable Snap To and the mouse will move to the default option in dialogue boxes.

HOT TIP: If you're not happy with how fast the pointer moves when you move your mouse, you can change that speed from the Pointer Options tab.

Change when the computer sleeps

Your computer is configured to go to sleep after a specific period of idle time. If you do not want your computer to go to sleep, for instance if Media Center is supposed to record something in the middle of the night, you can change this behaviour.

1 Click Start and in the Start Search window, type Power.

2 In the results, under Programs, click Power Options.

3 Click Change when the computer sleeps.

4 Use the drop-down lists to make changes as desired.

5 Click Save changes.

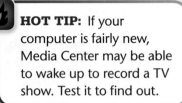

HOT TIP: If your computer is fairly new, Media Center may be able to wake up to record a TV show. Test it to find out.

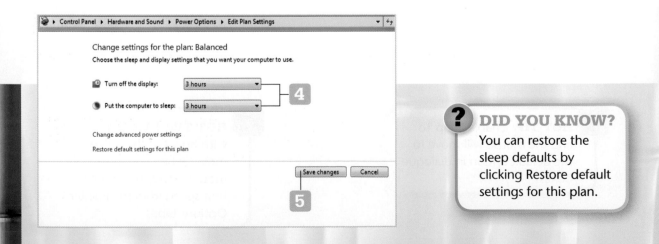

DID YOU KNOW?
You can restore the sleep defaults by clicking Restore default settings for this plan.

Change what happens when you press the Power button

Your computer is configured to do something specific when you press the Power button. By default, this is to shut down the computer but you can change this behaviour.

1 Click Start and in the Start Search window, type Power.

2 In the results, under Programs, click Power Options.

3 Click Choose what the power buttons do.

4 Use the drop-down lists to make changes as desired.

5 Click Save changes.

HOT TIP: You can change the settings so that pressing the Power button causes the computer to go to sleep.

ALERT: You can also require a password when the computer resumes from sleep to protect your PC from unauthorised access.

13 Create a HomeGroup and share data and printers

Introduction

Windows 7 lets you share data with other computers on your network. You can do this most simplistically by creating a HomeGroup on a private home network and having your other Windows 7 PCs join it. Once you've created a HomeGroup, you can easily share data, media, pictures and other items.

Important: HomeGroups only work to share data with other Windows 7 PCs. If you have XP or Vista PCs, you'll want to use the Public folders or create your own shared folders.

There are other ways to share data though – you can save or move data to the supplied Public folders for instance or you can create shared folders manually. You can also share printers and other hardware for use by others on your network or others who use your PC.

Locate the Public folders and create a desktop shortcut

You can share data with others on your network or those that share your PC from the Public folders. The Public folders are located on your local disk, generally C:, under Users, and in Public.

1 Click Start.

2 Click Computer.

3 Double-click Local Disk (C:) (or whatever letter represents your hard drive).

4 Double-click Users.

5 Right-click Public, click Send to: and click Desktop (create shortcut).

6 Close the Computer window.

◂ Hard Disk Drives (1)

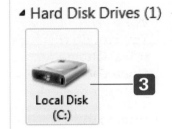

Local Disk (C:)

3

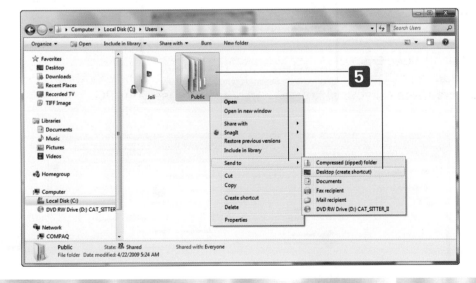

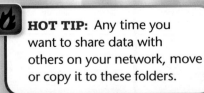

HOT TIP: If you share a computer, save the data you want to share in Public folders for easy access by other users.

HOT TIP: Any time you want to share data with others on your network, move or copy it to these folders.

Create a HomeGroup

You can share data in many ways using varying techniques. However, using a HomeGroup enables sharing the most easily. You create a HomeGroup in the Network and Sharing Center.

1 Open the Network and Sharing Center. (Click Start, in the Start Search window type Network and Sharing and click Network and Sharing Center.)

2 Click Ready to Create, by HomeGroup.

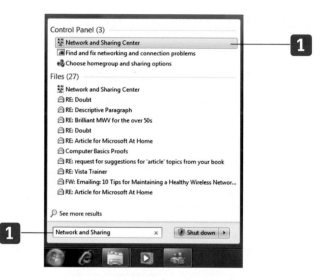

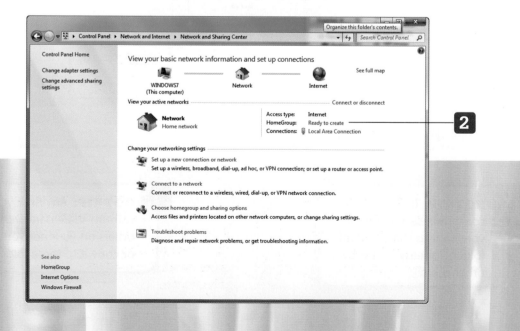

3 Click Create a homegroup.

4 Choose what you want to share and click Next.

5 Write down the password – you'll need it to allow other Windows 7 PCs to join the HomeGroup. Click Finish.

Control Panel ▶ Network and Internet ▶ HomeGroup · · · Search Control Panel

Share with other home computers running Windows 7

There is currently no homegroup on the network.

With a homegroup, you can share files and printers with other computers running Windows 7. You can also stream media to devices. The homegroup is protected with a password, and you'll always be able to choose what you share with the group.

Tell me more about homegroups

Change advanced sharing settings...

Start the HomeGroup troubleshooter

Create a homegroup   Cancel

3

Create a Homegroup

Share with other home computers running Windows 7

Your computer can share files and printers with other computers running Windows 7, and you can stream media to devices using a homegroup. The homegroup is protected with a password, and you'll always be able to choose what you share with the group.

Tell me more about homegroups

Select what you want to share:

☑ Pictures   ☐ Documents

4   ☑ Music   ☑ Printers

☑ Videos

4   Next   Cancel

HOT TIP: If you ever forget the password, simply open Network and Sharing Center, click Choose homegroup and sharing options, and click View or print the homegroup password.

ALERT: Computers must be running Windows 7 to participate in the HomeGroup. If you have other computers on your network that aren't running Windows 7, you'll want to share data using the Public Folders, detailed in this chapter.

Save data to the Public folders

To share data with anyone on your network or anyone who can also access your PC, save the data to share in the Public folders.

1 Open a picture, document or other item you wish to save to the Public folders.

2 Click File and click Save As.

3 In the Save As dialogue box, in the left pane, click Desktop. You'll then be able to double-click the Public shortcut you created earlier.

4 Select the Public subfolder to save to.

5 Type a name for the file.

6 Click Save.

HOT TIP: Save pictures to the Public Pictures folder. Save documents to the Public Documents folder.

ALERT: In Windows Photo Gallery, you'll click File and Make a Copy.

DID YOU KNOW?

It's actually better to move data you want to share into the Public folders. That way, you won't create duplicate copies of the data on your hard drive.

Copy or move data to the Public folder

You can access the Public folder by browsing to it. This may require you to browse the network if the Public folders are stored on another PC. However, if you put a shortcut to the Public folder on your desktop as detailed earlier in this chapter, you only need to double-click the folder to open it.

Once you have access to the Public folder you can drag items to the folder for sharing. As detailed in Chapter 4, it's best to right-click the data while dragging. That way, you can decide whether you want to copy the data or move it.

1 Open the Public folder.

2 Select the data you want to copy or move. You may have to position the two windows as shown here.

3 Select the data, right-click it and drag the Public folder.

4 Choose Copy Here, Move Here, or Create Shortcuts Here, as desired.

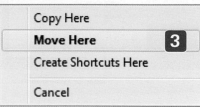

HOT TIP: In some circumstances, you won't be given the option Move Here. This happens when you are trying to move a default folder. In these instances, it's best to choose Create Shortcuts Here.

HOT TIP: When you can, configure data to save in the Public folders by default. For instance, have Media Center save all recorded TV here, not in your personal folders.

Share a personal folder

Sometimes you won't want to move or copy data into Public folders and subfolders. Instead, you'll want to share data directly from your personal folders. To do this, you'll have to manually share the desired personal folders.

1 Locate the folder to share.

2 Right-click the folder.

3 Choose Share with and click Homegroup. Choose Read to give users permission to view the files; choose Read/Write if you want users to be able to change the files too. Remember though, a HomeGroup can be joined only by other Windows 7 PCs. If you want to share with specific people who are not in a HomeGroup, choose Specific people.

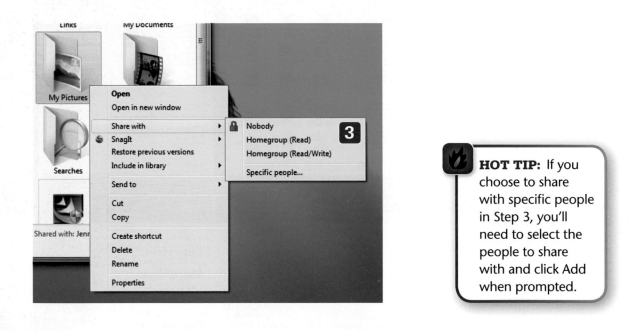

HOT TIP: If you choose to share with specific people in Step 3, you'll need to select the people to share with and click Add when prompted.

HOT TIP: You can apply advanced sharing options in the Network and Sharing Center, by clicking Choose homegroup and sharing options.

HOT TIP: You may want to share your own Pictures folder instead of copying or moving the files into the Public Pictures folder.

View a shared printer and/or add a printer

When you create a HomeGroup, printer sharing is automatically enabled. You can view shared printers from the Devices and Printers window in Windows 7 PCs. You can also add a printer that's connected to another PC from the Devices and Printers window. If you are not in a HomeGroup, you'll need to share your printers and devices manually.

1 Click Start and in the Start Search window, type Printers.

2 Under Control Panel, click View devices and printers.

3 Locate the shared printers. They will have a green tick beside them.

ALERT: Your PC and printer will need to be turned on for others to access the shared printer.

4 To add a printer, click Add a printer.

5 Locate the printer to add in the list and click Next. Continue to follow the prompts, as needed.

4

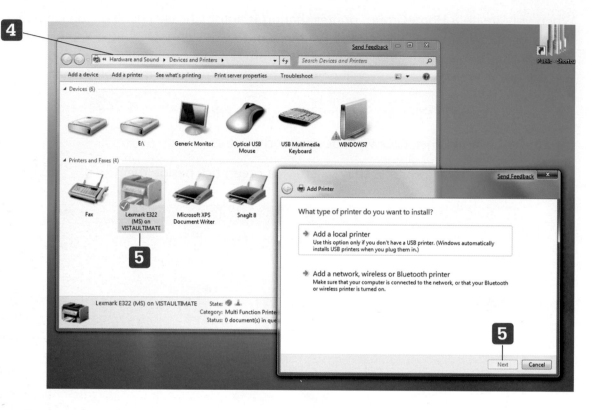

HOT TIP: To manually share a printer, right-click the printer and choose Printer Properties. From the Sharing tab, select the sharing options you desire.

HOT TIP: Right-click any printer to see its properties, what's printing and more.

ALERT: When others on your network access the printer for the first time, they may be prompted to install a driver for it. This is OK and will be managed by the PC.

14 Fix problems

Introduction

When problems arise, you will want to resolve them quickly. Windows 7 offers plenty of help. System Restore can fix problems automatically by 'restoring' your computer to an earlier time. If the boot-up process is slow, you can disable unwanted start-up items with the System Configuration tool. Additionally, you can use the Network and Sharing Center to help you resolve connectivity problems and use Device Manager to 'roll back' a driver that didn't work, and if your computer seems bogged down, you can delete unwanted programs and files easily.

Use System Restore

System Restore regularly creates and saves restore points that contain information about your computer that Windows uses to work properly. If your computer starts acting strangely, you can use System Restore to restore your computer to a time when the computer was working properly.

Open System Restore.

ALERT: System Restore can't be enabled unless the computer has at least 300 MB of free space on the hard disk, or if the disk is smaller than 1 GB.

WHAT DOES THIS MEAN?

Restore point: A snapshot of the Registry and system state that can be used to make an unstable computer stable again.

Registry: A part of the operating system that contains information about hardware configuration and settings, user configuration and preferences, software configuration and preferences, and other system-specific information.

2 Click Next.

3 Choose a restore point.

4 Click Finish.

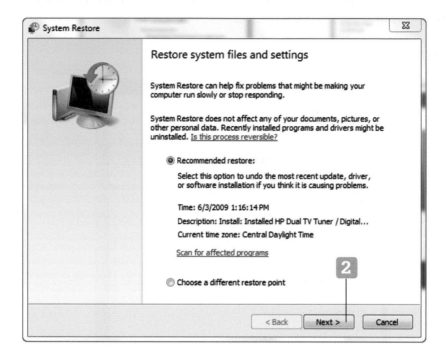

HOT TIP: Many problems occur due to loose or disconnected cables. A mouse can't work unless it's plugged in or its wireless component is. A cable modem can't work unless it's connected securely to the computer and the wall. When troubleshooting, always check your connections.

ALERT: If running System Restore on a laptop, make sure it's plugged it. System Restore should never be interrupted.

Disable unwanted start-up items

Lots of programs and applications start when you boot your computer. This causes the start-up process to take longer than it should and programs that start also run in the background, slowing down computer performance. You should disable unwanted start-up items to improve all-around performance.

1 Click Start.

2 In the Start Search window, type system configuration.

3 Under Programs, click System Configuration.

4 From the Startup tab, deselect third-party programs you recognise but do not use daily.

5 Click OK.

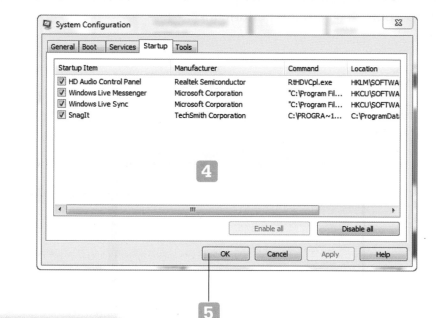

ALERT: You'll have to restart the computer to apply the changes.

ALERT: Do not deselect anything you don't recognise or the operating system!

Resolve Internet connectivity problems

When you have a problem connecting to your local network or to the Internet, you can often resolve the problem in the Network and Sharing Center.

1 Open the Network and Sharing Center.

2 Click the red X.

3 Perform the steps in the order they are presented.

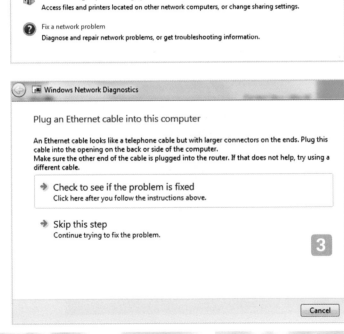

ALERT: If prompted to 'reset' your broadband or satellite connection, turn off all hardware, including the computer, and restart them in the following order: cable/satellite/DSL modem, router, computers.

? DID YOU KNOW?
Almost all of the time, performing the first step will resolve your network problem.

ALERT: When restarting a cable or satellite modem, remove any batteries to completely turn off the modem.

Use Device Driver Rollback

If you download and install a new driver for a piece of hardware and it doesn't work properly, you can use Device Driver Rollback to return to the previously installed driver.

1 Click Start.

2 Right-click Computer.

3 Click Properties.

4 Under Tasks, click Device Manager (not shown).

5 Click the + sign next to the hardware that uses the driver to rollback. It will change to a minus sign.

6 Double-click the device name.

7 Click the Driver tab and click Roll Back driver.

8 Click OK.

> **ALERT:** The Rollback driver option will be available only if a new driver has recently been installed.

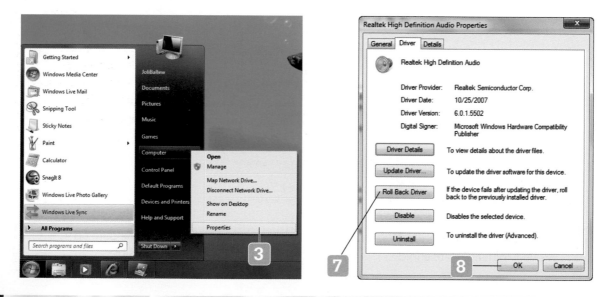

? DID YOU KNOW?
Many items of hardware have multiple connections and connection types. If one type of connection doesn't work, like USB, try FireWire.

! ALERT: You can rollback only to the previous driver. This means that if you have a driver (D) and then install a new driver (D1) and it doesn't work, and then you install another driver (D2) and it doesn't work, using Device Driver Rollback will revert to D1, not the driver (D) before it.

View available hard drive space

Problems can occur when hard drive space gets too low. This can become a problem when you use a computer to record television shows or movies (these require a lot of hard drive space) or if your hard drive is partitioned.

1 Click Start.

2 Click Computer.

3 In the Computer window, right-click the C: drive and choose Properties.

4 View the available space.

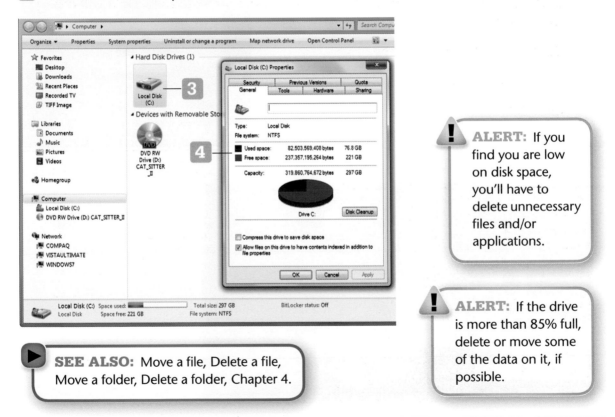

ALERT: If you find you are low on disk space, you'll have to delete unnecessary files and/or applications.

ALERT: If the drive is more than 85% full, delete or move some of the data on it, if possible.

▶ **SEE ALSO:** Move a file, Delete a file, Move a folder, Delete a folder, Chapter 4.

WHAT DOES THIS MEAN?

Partition: Some hard drives are configured to have multiple sections, called partitions. The C: partition may have 20 GB available, while the D: partition may have 60 GB. If you save everything to the C: partition (failing to use the D: partition), it can get full quickly.

Delete unwanted Media Center media

One of the places you'll find data that hogs disk space is in Media Center's storage areas. This is especially true if you record television programmes or movies or create your own movies. TV and movies take up a lot of hard drive space.

1 Open Media Center.

2 Under TV + Movies, click recorded tv.

3 Right-click any recording and click Delete.

4 Repeat as necessary.

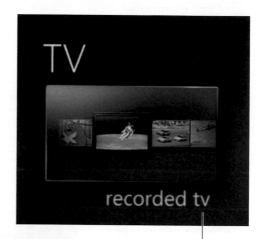

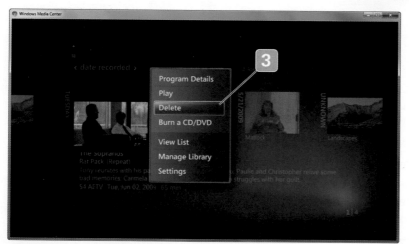

2

Uninstall unwanted programs

If you haven't used an application in more than a year, you probably never will. You can uninstall unwanted programs from the Control Panel.

1 Click Start, click Control Panel.

2 In Control Panel, click Uninstall a program.

3 Scroll through the list. Click a program name if you want to uninstall it.

4 Click Uninstall.

5 Follow the prompts to uninstall the program.

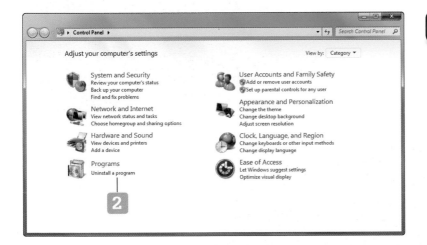

HOT TIP: Look for programs in the list that start with the name of the manufacturer of your computer (Acer, Hewlett-Packard, Dell, etc.) Some you may want to keep, but it's best to uninstall what you don't need.

ALERT: Your computer may have come with programs you don't even know about. Perform these steps to find out.

Top 10 Windows 7 Problems Solved

Problem 1. My computer seems bogged down. What can I do?

Disk Cleanup is a safe and effective way to reduce unnecessary data on your PC. With unnecessary data deleted, your PC will run faster and have more available disk space for saving files and installing programs. With Disk Cleanup you can remove temporary files, empty the Recycle Bin, remove set-up log files and downloaded program files (among other things), all in a single process.

1 Click Start.

2 In the Start Search dialogue box, type Disk Cleanup.

3 In the results, under Programs, click Disk Cleanup.

ALERT: You may not be prompted to choose a drive letter if only one drive exists.

4 If prompted to choose a drive or partition, choose the letter of the drive that contains the operating system, which is almost always C: but occasionally D:. Click OK.

5 Select the files to delete. Accept the defaults if you aren't sure.

6 Click OK to start the cleaning process.

ALERT: If you empty the Recycle Bin all files will be permanently deleted.

Problem 2. I created a file a while back and now can't locate it. How can I find it?

After you create data, you save it to your hard drive. When you're ready to use the file again, you have to locate it and open it. There are several ways to locate a saved file. If you know the document is in the Documents folder, you can click Start and then click Documents. Then you can simply double-click the file to open it. However, if you aren't sure where the file is, you can search for it from the Start menu.

1 Click Start.

2 In the Start Search window, type the name of the file.

3 Click the file to open it. There will be multiple search results.

Documents (2)
- ♪ My First Sound Recording
- My First Text Document

Videos (1)
- My First Windows DVD Maker Project

Files (482)
- FW: Bridal Shower First Thoughts
- Bridal Shower First Thoughts
- RE: Bridal Shower First Thoughts
- RE: First 33 pages
- FW: First 33 pages
- RE: First 33 pages
- RE: First 33 pages
- Bridal Shower First Thoughts
- RE: Windows Vista Question
- Help protect your phone's information with My Phone

🔎 See more results

2 First × | Shut down ▶

? DID YOU KNOW?
If you don't know any part of the name of the file, you can type a word that is included inside the file or a specific type of file.

! ALERT: If you don't know the exact name of the file, you can type part of the name.

Problem 3. I can't connect to the Internet although I could yesterday. What can I do?

If you are having trouble connecting to the Internet through a public or private network, you can diagnose Internet problems using the Network and Sharing Center.

1 Open the Network and Sharing Center.

2 To diagnose a non-working Internet connection, click Troubleshoot problems.

3 Select an option that describes your problem.

4 Work through the troubleshooter to resolve the problem.

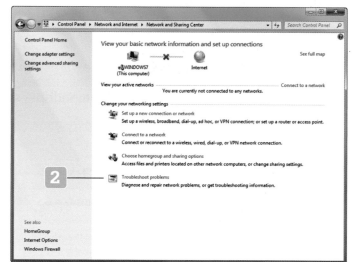

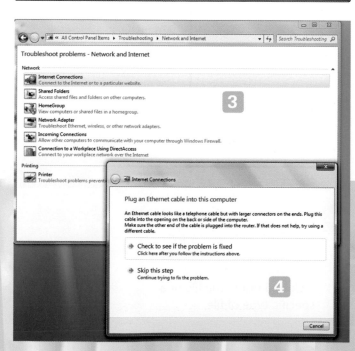

Problem 4. Where is the e-mail program? I can't find Outlook Express or Windows Mail.

Windows 7 doesn't come with an e-mail program – you have to download and install Windows Live Mail.

1 Open Internet Explorer and go to http://www.windowslive.com/mail.

2 Look for the Download now button and click it. You'll be prompted to click Download now once more on the next screen.

3 Click Run and when prompted, click Yes.

4 When prompted, select the items to download. You can select all of the items, some of the items or only Mail. Then click Install.

5 When prompted to select your settings, make the desired choices. You can't go wrong here – there are no bad options.

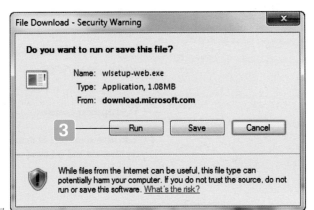

Problem 5. I get a lot of junk e-mail. How can I stop it from coming in?

Just like you receive unwanted information from estate agents, radio stations and television ads, you're going to get unwanted advertisements in e-mails. This is referred to as junk e-mail or spam. Most of these advertisements are scams and rip-offs and they also often contain pornographic images. There are four filtering options in Windows Live Mail: No Automatic Filtering, Low, High, and Safe List Only.

1 In Windows Live Mail, click the Menus icon.

2 Click Safety options.

3 From the Options tab, select a Junk Mail filtering option.

4 Click OK.

ALERT: Never buy anything from a junk e-mail, send money to a non-registered charity, send money for your portion of a lottery ticket or fall for other spam hoaxes.

ALERT: Don't give your email address to any website or company, or include it in any registration card, unless you're willing to receive junk email from them and their constituents.

Problem 6. I want my kids to have access, but only on my terms. What can I do?

If you share the PC with someone, everyone should have their own personal account. If every person who accesses your PC has their own standard user account and password, and if every person logs on using that account and then logs off the PC each time they've finished using it, you'll never have to worry about anyone accessing anyone else's personal data.

1 Click Start.

2 Click Control Panel.

3 Click Add or remove user accounts.

4 Click Create a new account.

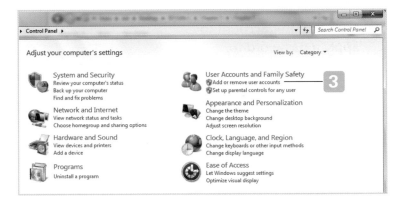

? DID YOU KNOW?

When you need to make a system-wide change, you have to be logged on as an administrator or type an administrator's user name and password.

Guest
Guest account is off

Create a new account —— **4**

What is a user account?

Additional things you can do

Set up Parental Controls

Go to the main User Accounts page

? DID YOU KNOW?

Administrators can make changes to system-wide settings but standard users cannot (without an administrator name and password).

5 Type a new account name, verify Standard user is selected and click Create Account.

Now, add passwords to all of the accounts:

6 Click Start.

7 Click Control Panel.

8 Click Add or remove user accounts.

9 Click the user account to apply a password to.

10 Click Create a password.

11 Type the new password, type it again to confirm it and type a password hint.

12 Click Create password.

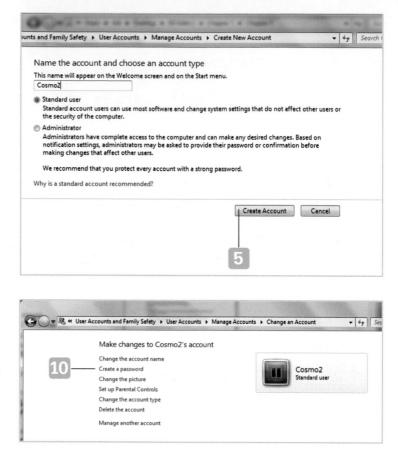

ounts and Family Safety ▸ User Accounts ▸ Manage Accounts ▸ Create New Account

Name the account and choose an account type

This name will appear on the Welcome screen and on the Start menu.

Cosmo2

◉ Standard user
Standard account users can use most software and change system settings that do not affect other users or the security of the computer.

○ Administrator
Administrators have complete access to the computer and can make any desired changes. Based on notification settings, administrators may be asked to provide their password or confirmation before making changes that affect other users.

We recommend that you protect every account with a strong password.

Why is a standard account recommended?

Create Account   Cancel

5

« User Accounts and Family Safety ▸ User Accounts ▸ Manage Accounts ▸ Change an Account

Make changes to Cosmo2's account

Change the account name
Create a password
Change the picture
Set up Parental Controls
Change the account type
Delete the account

Manage another account

Cosmo2
Standard user

10

« User Accounts ▸ Manage Accounts ▸ Change an Account ▸ Create Password   Search Control Panel

Create a password for Cosmo2's account

Cosmo2
Standard user

You are creating a password for Cosmo2.

If you do this, Cosmo2 will lose all EFS-encrypted files, personal certificates and stored passwords for Web sites or network resources.

To avoid losing data in the future, ask Cosmo2 to make a password reset floppy disk.

New password
Confirm new password
If the password contains capital letters, they must be typed the same way every time.
How to create a strong password

Type a password hint
The password hint will be visible to everyone who uses this computer.
What is a password hint?

11   **12**

Create password   Cancel

ALERT: Create a password that contains upper- and lower-case letters and a few numbers. Write the password down and keep it somewhere out of sight and safe.

Problem 7. I was on a website and got pop-ups about viruses. How can I find out if I really have a virus?

If you think your computer has been attacked by an Internet threat (virus, worm, malware, etc.) you can run a manual scan using Windows Defender.

1 Open Windows Defender. (Click Start, type Windows Defender, and under Control Panel click Windows Defender.)

2 Click the arrow next to Scan (not the Scan icon). Click Full scan if you think the computer has been infected.

3 Click the X in the top right corner to close the Windows Defender window.

Control Panel (2)

Windows Defender

Scan for spyware and other potentially unwanted software

1

See more results

Windows Defender ✕   Shut down ▶

2   **3**

Windows Defender

Home   Scan ▾   History   Tools   ? ▾

Protection against spyware and pote...

Quick scan
Full scan   **2**
Custom scan...
Cancel scan

Last scan:
Not available

Status

Last scan:	Not available
Scan schedule:	Daily around 2:00 AM (Quick scan)
Real-time protection:	On
Antispyware definitions:	Version 1.65.146.0 created on 8/31/2009 at 2:46 AM

Problem 8. I keep seeing warnings about security issues. Where can I learn more?

Windows 7 tries hard to take care of your PC and your data. You'll see a pop-up if your anti-virus software is out of date (or not installed), if you don't have the proper security settings configured or if Windows Update or the firewall is disabled. You'll also get a user account control prompt each time you want to install a program or make a system-wide change.

1 Open the Action Center. (Click Start and type Action Center.)

2 If there's anything in red or yellow, click the down arrow (if necessary) to see the problem.

3 Click View problem response to view the resolution and perform the task.

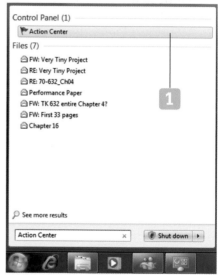

Problem 9. How can I create a schedule and back up my data?

Windows 7 comes with a backup program you can use to back up your personal data. The backup program is located in the Backup and Restore Center.

1 Open the Backup and Restore Center.

2 Click Set up backup. (Once it's set up, the button will change to Back up now.)

3 Choose a place to save your backup. Click Next.

Back up or restore user and system files

Backup

Windows Backup has not been set up.

[Set up backup...]

Restore

Windows could not find a backup for this computer.

Select another backup to restore files from

You can use the Recovery Control Panel to restore your computer to an earlier date.

2

Configure Backup

Select where you want to save your backup

We recommend that you save your backup on an external hard drive. Guidelines for choosing a backup destination

Backup locations:

Drive	Free Space	Total Size
DVD RW Drive (D:)		

[Refresh]   [Add network location...]

System images cannot be saved on this device. (More information)
The backed up data cannot be securely protected for this device. (More information)

3   [Next] [Cancel]

? DID YOU KNOW?

You may be prompted to insert a blank DVD or insert a USB drive depending on the choice made in Step 3.

4 Select Let Windows choose (recommended), then click Next.

5 Wait while the backup completes.

What do you want to back up?

4

○ Let Windows choose (recommended)

Windows will back up data files saved in libraries, on the desktop, and in default Windows folders. These items will be backed up on a regular schedule. How does Windows choose what files to back up?

○ Let me choose

You can select libraries and folders and whether to include a system image in the backup. The items you choose will be backed up on a regular schedule.

Next   Cancel

4

? DID YOU KNOW?

You can't create a backup on the hard disk of the computer you are backing up.

🔥 HOT TIP: Since backups can be large, consider a USB drive, external hard drive or DVD. You can also choose a network location.

Problem 10. Yesterday my computer started acting up. What is the first step I should take?

The first step in resolving any computer problem is to use System Restore. System Restore regularly creates and saves restore points that contain information about your computer that Windows uses to work properly. If your computer starts acting strangely, you can use System Restore to restore your computer to a time when the computer was working properly.

1 Open System Restore.

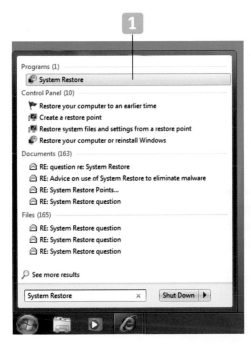

> **HOT TIP:** Many problems occur due to loose or disconnected cables. A mouse can't work unless it's plugged in or its wireless component is. A cable modem can't work unless it's connected securely to the computer and the wall. When troubleshooting, always check your connections.

2 Click Next to accept and apply the recommended restore point.

3 Click Finish.

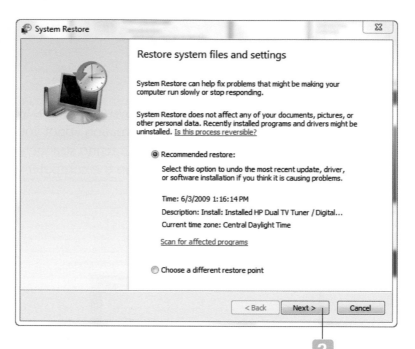

2

ALERT: If running System Restore on a laptop, make sure it's plugged it. System Restore should never be interrupted.

? DID YOU KNOW?
Because System Restore works only with its own system files, running System Restore will not affect any of your personal data. Your pictures, email, documents, music, etc. will not be deleted or changed.